Introduction to Brain-Compatible Learning

Eric Jensen

Introduction to Brain-Compatible Learning

Eric Jensen

Dedication
To you who are just getting started. May you enjoy both the journey and the results. Many thanks to my wife Diane for her priceless support.

Editing: Karen Markowitz
Cover Design and Layout: Tracy Sciacca

ISBN #1-890460-00-1

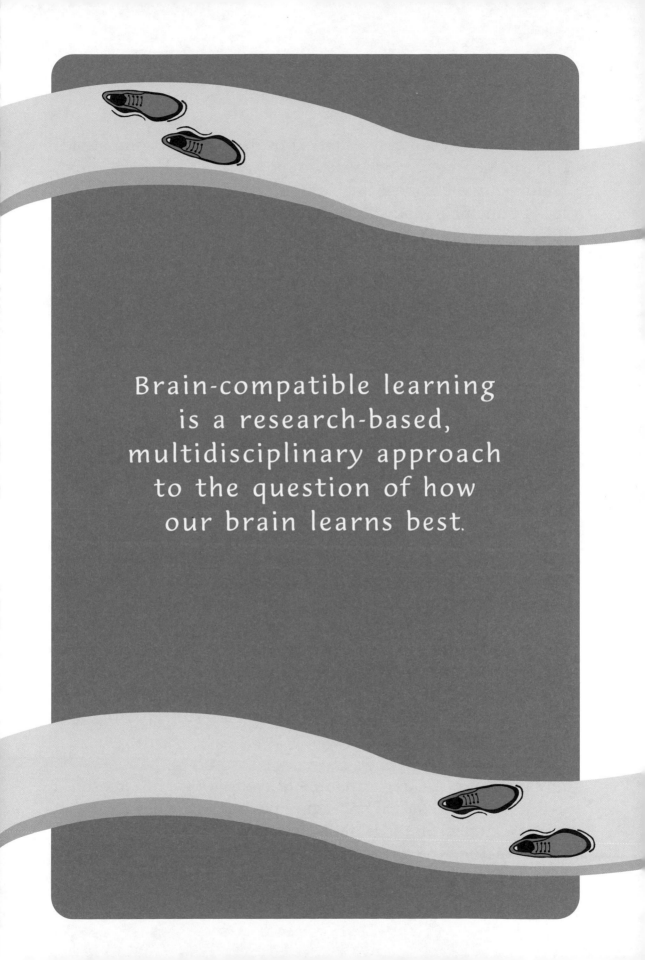

Brain-compatible learning
is a research-based,
multidisciplinary approach
to the question of how
our brain learns best.

Introduction

In June of 1980, I got my first exposure to "brain-compatible" learning. The impact was so powerful, that even today, almost two decades later, I can fill up a flip chart page with ideas I remember (and still use) from that workshop! The facilitators clearly understood some important principles about the brain. I became so enthusiastic (some would say a zealot) that I decided to share this excitement with others. Since I was teaching at that time, my first response was, "Why don't my own students have this experience everyday?" It was both humbling and promising.

This newfound brain-learning connection became my springboard for innovation. Soon after the workshop I co-founded an experimental cutting-edge academic program called SuperCamp. The purpose was to empower teens with life skills and learning tools using the latest research on the brain. We held our first SuperCamp session in August of 1982. It was an immediate success and sessions were soon spread to other states and countries. We were flooded with media attention and found ourselves covered in *USA Today*, *The Wall Street Journal* and later, on *CNN* and *Good Morning America*. Long term follow-up research validated that the benefits of the program lasted years after the ten-day program itself. Grades and participation in school were up; and students reported greater self confidence. The experiment we began years ago is now an international fixture with over 20,000 graduates. Today, it's still growing and based in Oceanside, California.

I am a zealot of brain-compatible learning for a good reason. I have seen, felt and heard first-hand the difference these learning principles make. Students of all backgrounds, with every imaginable history of failure, of every age and attitude of discouragement can and have succeeded with this approach.

While this approach is not a panacea, it does provide some important directions as we move into the twenty-first century. Programs that are compatible with the way humans naturally learn will stand the test of time. Though brain-compatible learning has been "proven" by teachers in real world classrooms for years, it's gratifying to find that after years of research, the brain has now also "made it" onto the honored shelves of the academic elite.

This book is written for you - the classroom teacher, trainer, administrator, lifelong learner - you, a catalyst for doing the all-important work of facilitating learning the best way possible. The intent of this book is to introduce you to the basics of this exciting paradigm shift in education. If at the end you have a good grasp of the core differences between the traditional approach and the brain-compatible approach to learning, and a framework for understanding the 12 principles presented, I will have satisfied my objective. If at the end you are also thinking "Okay.... What's Next?", I will be elated. For then, I will have successfully passed on my passion for learning in a brain-compatible way. This should be a painless and fun adventure... Follow the trail signs and you will surely learn along the way.

Eric Jensen

Table of Contents

Section One

Two

Three   Two Continued

Trail Guide to Brain-Compatible Awareness:
Section 1

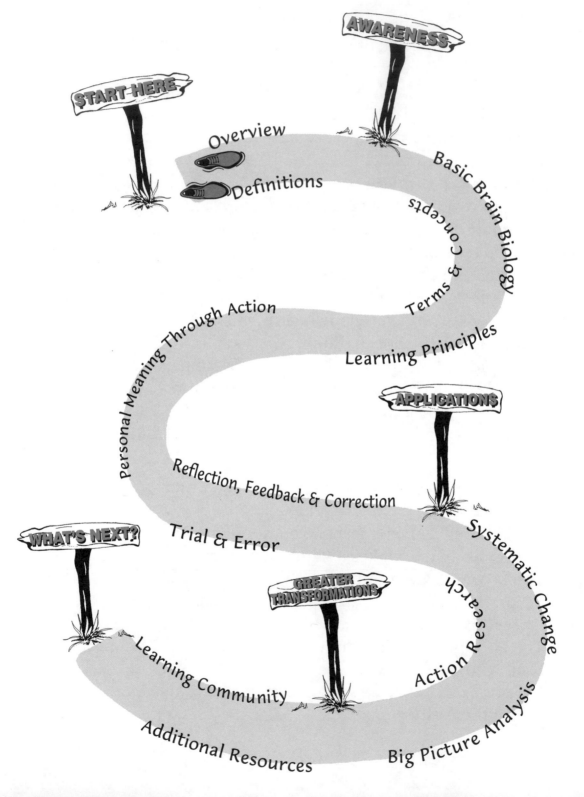

AWARENESS

START HERE

Overview

Definitions

Basic Brain Biology

Terms & Concepts

Personal Meaning Through Action

Learning Principles

APPLICATIONS

Reflection, Feedback & Correction

WHAT'S NEXT?

Trial & Error

Systematic Change

GREATER TRANSFORMATIONS

Learning Community

Action Research

Additional Resources

Big Picture Analysis

What Is Brain-Compatible Learning?

Good question. Let's explore it a bit. The first form of schooling was simple. It was the apprenticeship method. For most of human history, if you wanted to learn about something, you'd find someone better at it than you and learn from them. This worked for centuries.

Then, the industrial revolution hatched a new model. It was the notion that you could bring everyone together in a single place and offer a standardized, conveyor-belt curriculum. This second model or paradigm of schooling was developed in the 1800s and popularized through most of the twentieth century. It is often called "The Factory Model." Factory skills like obedience, orderliness, unity and respect for authority were emphasized.

As we entered the information age from 1950 to 1980, schools moved away from the factory model and became organized around two main objectives: controlling the flow of information and socialization. We'll call this the "control model." During this era, we were also influenced by educational doctrines from the social sciences. The behaviorist-linked theories that permeated this era (and still linger) go something like this: "We don't know what goes on inside the brain, so let's measure behaviors, and modify them with behavior-reinforcers. If we like it, reward it. If we don't, punish it."Other philosophical concepts of the time included the "demand model", "sage-on-the-stage", and "stand-and-deliver." That is, learners were expected to answer teacher questioning "on demand"; and the teacher was considered the "expert" whose job it was to impart "knowledge" from the front of the classroom. Considering what we knew about the brain at that time, this approach made some sense.

A new paradigm was soon to emerge, however. For the first time in history, through the use of discoveries in medical technology, we could measure the brain while its owner was still alive. A whole different breed of "inner science" was developing called neuroscience; not a single discipline, but an exciting interdisciplinary approach to understanding the brain. Neuroscience draws from chemistry, immunology, biology, pharmacology, computational sciences, medicine, systems thinking and artificial intelligence modeling. Based on this synergy of disciplines, the third educational paradigm in two thousand years began to take shape. This exciting interdisciplinary approach to learning is known as brain-based or brain-compatible learning .

Taken in pieces, this emerging movement is incoherent. Taken as a whole, brain-compatible learning is impressive. It will change our school start times, discipline policies, methods of assessment, teaching strategies, budget priorities, classroom environments, use of technology and even the way we think of arts and physical education.

At first glance, brain-compatible learning might seem like a lot of biology or principles that are mere platitudes on learning theory. But upon closer examination educators are realizing that having "hard science" to support our successful classroom practices (ones we knew worked, but were hard to "prove") arms us with a greater degree of professionalism. The science of how the brain learns best is a revolution in learning - a transformation that will help us do a better job of reaching all students.

There are countless real-life personal and peer applications for the information in this book to insure your success. You must try out these concepts for yourself for it is in applying the learning that you will begin to fully understand brain-based learning. Once you experience it, the natural inclination is to want to share it with your students and colleagues.

A larger systems application of brain-compatible learning is ultimately where we are headed. When whole schools and districts have reassessed their thinking about learning, their curriculums, assessment methods, and school structures; and implemented brain-based strategies at this level, we will truly have reformed our educational institutions. Until we make research, reflection, and renewal, as basic to schools as are the "3 R's", our learning strategies will be less than optimal. As individual teachers, trainers and administrators move towards the new paradigm, eventually, everyone will benefit.

The following questions are addressed as you make your way along the Brain-Compatible Trail throughout this guide.

- Does comparing one learner to another make sense?
- How are learners impacted by high stress and threat?
- How do windows of opportunity influence learners?
- When is it easiest to learn foreign languages?
- Why should fruit, protein, and nuts be in campus vending machines?
- Why are the phrases "on task" or "off task" irrelevant?
- Does the brain ever stop growing?
- What constitutes an enriched learning environment?
- How can we ensure students receive enough feedback?
- Why purposely engage strong emotions every day?
- Is no-stress learning the best kind?
- How can we get kids to remember more of what they learn?
- Why do kids tend not to pay attention in class?
- Why don't you want learners' attention most of the time?
- Why should school starting times be changed?
- Why post mind-maps of whole units weeks in advance?
- Why is group work or cooperative learning good for the brain?
- To what degree does our brain change over time?
- In what ways does a brain-compatible curriculum boost student motivation?
- Why should rewards be eliminated from schools?

The Old
and New of It

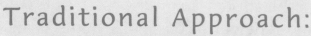

Old

Traditional Approach:

Behaviorist Model
Control Model
Reductionist Thinking
The Demand Model
Sage on the Stage

Common Strategies:

Identify Goals for Students
Demand Students Learn
Stand and Deliver
Reward Desired Behaviors
Punish Negative Behaviors

New

Brain-Compatible Approach:

Theories Embraced
Choices (versus Control)
Possibility Thinking
Holistic/Systems Approach
Bio-complexity Model

Common Strategies:

Learner Input
Threat-free Enrichment
Intrinsic Motivation
Multi-disciplinary/age/level/modality learning
Working With Whole Systems

When Brain Research Is Applied to the Classroom, It Impacts:

- Discipline Policies

- Curriculum

- New Teacher Training

- Classroom Design

- Grouping/Sorting

- Scheduling

- Instructional Strategies

- Assessment

- Budget Priorities

- Staff Development

- Food Service Programs

- Technology

- Bilingual Programs

- Special Education

We're Not in Kansas Anymore

We need to be aware of the tendency to do things in a particular way just because that's the way we've always done them. But we also need to beware of the *"It's got to be new or it's not any good"* syndrome.

If pieces of the brain-compatible approach sound familiar to you, they are. But the pieces do not equal the available synergy. Avoid being lured into a false sense of familiarity.

It's not another fad; it's not "ho-hum" business as usual. Taken as a whole, this approach provides a fundamentally different stage on which learning can be orchestrated.

Change Can Be Easy!

Remember, dramatic change can come from:

- Taking advantage of something you know about, but don't do.

- Eliminating something that's useless or harmful.

- Being willing to "not know"; to start over and learn anew.

- Doing much more of something that you already do.

Where's the Proof?

Research on the brain does not necessarily "prove" that something is a good classroom strategy. That's too big of a leap to make. But the research can support and illuminate strategies already in use, steer us in the right direction, and help us to avoid some highly inappropriate strategies. How can research do this? Scientists are paving this new ground with rapidly changing technological advances. Tomorrow's tools will be even more sophisticated, but here is a sampling of some common ones used currently:

FMRI - Functional Magnetic Resonance Imaging provides high quality cross-sectional images of soft tissue without X-rays or radiation.

Animals - Lab experiments done with rats, dogs, cats, slugs, apes, etc. provide a rich source of information about how similar brains work. For example, we have learned much about the role of enriched environments from studying rat brains.

Computerized Electrodes (EEG and MEG) - These tools give readings about the electrical output of the brain. They've been used to detect brain wave patterns that represent various brain states and abnormal cerebral function such as seizures or dementia. These tools can also help us track, for example, how much activity is going on during problem-solving.

Clinical Studies - Using human volunteers, often from university psychology classes, we can learn much. For example, flashing slides at high speeds can tell us about reaction times of the visual system.

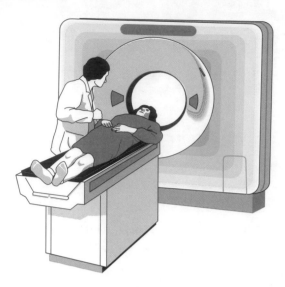

PET - Positron Emission Tomography is an imaging device. It begins with giving the subject a drink of "spiked" water (015) or radioactive glucose. Then it reads the amount of radioactive substances (positrons - the antimatter to electrons) released when certain areas of the brain consume glucose through usage.

Autopsies - Weight, stages of development, amount of decay or lesions can all be observed or measured by a neurological pathologist. Using autopsies, University of California, Los Angeles neuroscientist Bob Jacobs discovered that students who had more challenging and demanding school lives had more dendritic branching (which some say represents a type of intelligence) than those who didn't.

Spectrometers - These devices measure the specifics of brain chemical movement as an activity is happening. For example, if I'm feeling depressed, a spectrometer measurement can tell me if there's been a change in the levels of specific neurotransmitters in my frontal lobes.

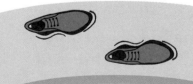

10 Reasons to Care About Recent Brain Research

Ten:

Everybody has a brain, so this field includes everyone you work with and live with.

Nine:

It's already talked about in the everyday news. More people are getting familiar with the research. You might as well join in and take advantage of it.

Eight:

The new renaissance of brain research is now. You could personally meet the next DaVinci, Einstein, or Curie.

Seven:

It can help you get ahead in life. You could become much smarter or have a way better memory.

Six:

The brain is 2 percent of your body's weight but uses 20 percent of your body's energy. Shouldn't you know where all that energy goes?

Five:

The 1990s are "The Decade of the Brain." Sale ends soon!

Four:

You might discover some really useful things: how to lower stress at work, how to boost learning and engage your learners.

Three:

You are losing thousands of brain cells every day. Find out what to do about that.

Two:

You could find out why some students don't learn as well as others and learn what to do about it.

One:

We will *all* get old someday. The older you live, the greater the likelihood of diseases like Alzheimer's or Parkinson's. Then, you'll *really* care about it!

The Evolution of Learning

Primitive models on the workings of the brain have been around for two thousand years. The brain has been referred to as a hydraulic system (the Greco-Roman model), a fluid system (Renaissance), an enchanted loom (the early Industrial Revolution), a city's switchboard (early to mid-1900s) and a computer (1950s and on).

The split-brain theory of the 1970s told us that we just needed more right-brained or whole brain learning. The hologram model (1980s) said everything was everywhere in the brain.

The triune brain theory (1970s and 1980s) introduced the three-part evolutionary-based schema that told us survival learning was in the lower-brain, emotions were in the mid-brain, and higher order thinking in the upper-brain area.

The reductionist/mechanistic model said that if you could isolate any individual part of the brain, you could understand its function and value to the system. As an example, our emotional responses were isolated in the amygdala.

The current biocomplexity model (1990s) espouses that every structure in the brain has some relational connectivity (physical, chemical, electrical or peripheral) to another. This model embraces the body-mind as a second circuit for information exchange. The peptides (amino acids) found throughout the body are just as important for information exchange as the brain's other system of neuronal connectivity - synapses. In short, the days of "What does this part of the brain do?" are diminishing. We now know that the brain's functioning often depends on the specific situation, emotions present at the time, the age of the person, their health, and their past experiences. We are realizing just how complex the brain really is!

Be a Brain-Smart Consumer:
Recognizing Good Research

Rating scale from one star (worst) to four stars (best)

Clinical Studies

(Good stuff!)
Usually university-supported and conducted with multiple experimenters, double-blind design, large, diverse, multi-age, multi-cultural populations.

"In Context" Studies

(Rare but good!)
Done in schools or businesses, this documented action research gives us testing results under actual, real-life conditions.

Discovery Studies

(Be curious!)
This is the hard science department. Could come from autopsies, experiments, FMRI, PET or EEG scans. This should get your interest, but it's not the final word.

Brain Theory

(Be cautious!)
Any theory about learning and the brain that explains recurring behaviors may be overly simplistic. Theories are usually made up by famous people but they might not be true. Examples include the triune or holographic brain models.

Action or Theory:
Who Wants to Read All That Research?

Yes, it can get a bit technical-especially when they're talking about post-traumatic lesions in the anterior medial temporal lobe resulting in retrograde amnesia. AAAAHH! But relax. You don't have to know all these words.

First, there's only a small percentage of brain research that carries with it useful applications for educators. Much of it is highly esoteric or pathology (disease) oriented. Brain research isn't usually directed at traditional learning; however, it can suggest ideas or educational paths that have a higher probability of success. A great deal of action or applied research in the classroom is still needed. A great deal of what's useful and what's not will come from thoughtful educators like yourself who take the lab research concept seriously and turn it into action research.

Second, there's only a dozen or so principles that make up the brain-compatible learning paradigm. When applied correctly, these principles will revolutionize learning and education. Yet, it's not how much you know about the brain that matters, it's how much you apply!

Take what you learn and experiment with it. Keep a journal, reflect, share, dialogue, consider feedback, and correct. You don't need a pile of scholarly research (although much of it is very interesting!) to make a big difference in your students' lives. One educator said, "As a country, we do more educational research than anyone else in the world, and we ignore more of it as well." It is the action or application of the research that we need in our classrooms, not theory. With the basic knowledge you are acquiring right now, you will be equipped to apply the research.

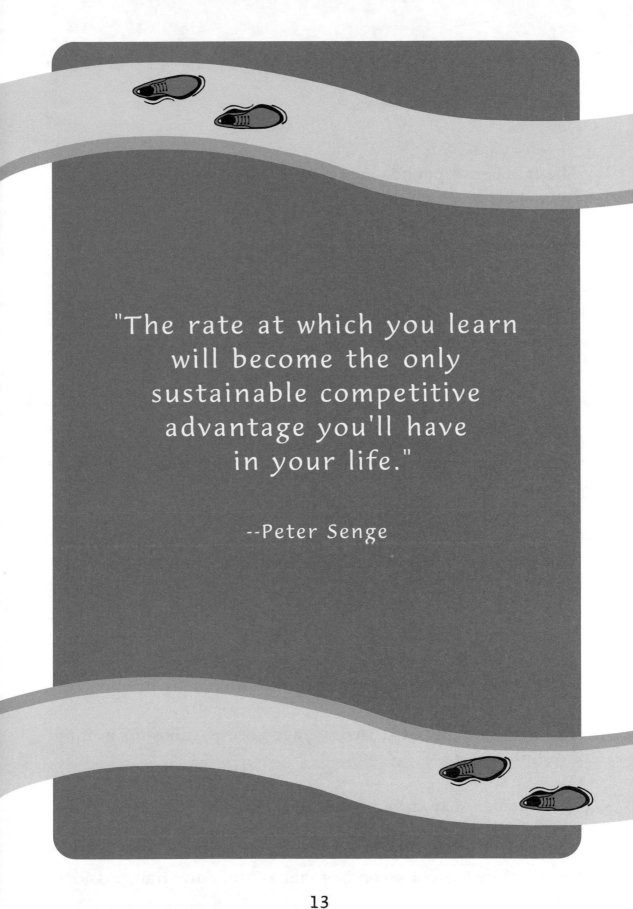

"The rate at which you learn
will become the only
sustainable competitive
advantage you'll have
in your life."

--Peter Senge

Fun Factoids On the Brain

3 and 1350 ...

The number of pounds and grams, respectively that the adult human brain weighs

17 and 7,800 ...

The number of pounds and grams, respectively, that the adult sperm whale brain weighs

7 ...

The percentage that the average male brain is larger in size than the average female brain

7 ...

The percentage that the average male body size is larger than the female

4 ...

The average weight, in pounds, of a dolphin brain

1 ...

The average weight of a gorilla brain in pounds

540 ...

The average number of square inches of the "unfolded" human cortex

4 ...

The number of lobes of the human brain

1,000,000 ...

The number of nerve fibers in the adult human brain

13 ...

The age, in years, that the average corpus callosum is fully myelinated

1 ...

The number of synaptic connections between our nose and the amygdala

100 ...

Speed, in meters per second, of the fastest neural transmissions

2 ...

The average percentage of your own brain's weight versus your body weight

78 ...

The average percentage of water, by weight that the human brain is made of

6 ...

The number of different layers in the cerebral cortex

1,000,000,000,000 ...

The estimated number of glial (support cells) in a human brain

2 ...

The estimated percent of the brain-body communication that occurs at the synaptic level (the rest is through widely dispersed peptide molecules)

100 ...

The number, in billions, of neurons in an average adult brain

50 ...

The number of chemical messengers (neurotransmitters) identified so far

10 ...

The average percentage of fat, by weight, that the human brain is made of

8 ...

The average percentage of protein, by weight, that the human brain is made of

70 ...

The percent by volume that the cortex makes up of the entire brain

.25 ...

The thickness, in inches, of our neocortex

1,000,000,000,000 ...

Typical number of connections in a newborn's brain

50,000,000,000,000 ...

The number of synaptic connections in an adult's brain

Brain Biology 101

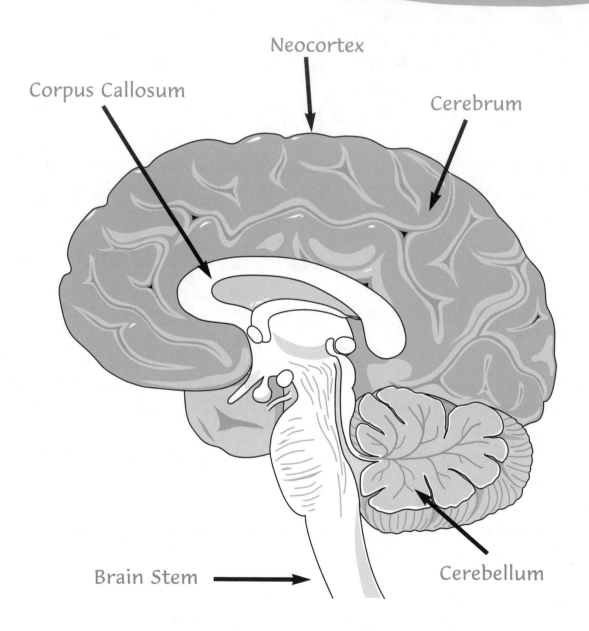

Neocortex

Corpus Callosum

Cerebrum

Cerebellum

Brain Stem

Brain Graphic By LifeART

Lobe Locations of the Human Brain

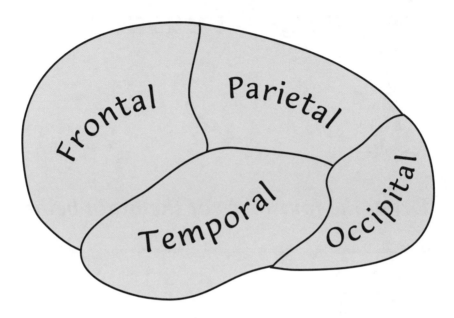

Frontal (judgment, creativity, decision-making, planning)

Parietal (higher sensory, language, short-term memory)

Temporal (language, writing, hearing, sensory associations, memory)

Occipital (receives and processes visual information)

Scientists divide the brain into four areas called lobes. They are occipital, frontal, parietal and temporal. The occipital lobe is in the middle back of the brain. It's primarily responsible for vision. The frontal lobe is the area around your forehead. It's involved with purposeful acts like judgment, creativity, problem-solving and planning. The parietal lobe is on the top back area. It's duties include processing higher sensory and language functions. The temporal lobes (left and right side) are above and around the ears. These areas are primarily responsible for hearing, memory, meaning and language. There is some overlap in the functions of the lobes.

Brain Teaser:

Draw the four lobes of the brain below.

The Brain Divided:
Right-Left Hemispheres

The Brain Has Two Hemispheres...
The Left and Right Cerebrum (also known as cortex). The Neocortex (a 1/4 inch thick wrinkled skin-like tissue layer) covers the cerebrum (see page 16).

The Corpus Callosum...
Is a bundle of nerve tissue (about 250 million nerves) connecting the left and right brain hemispheres (See page 16).

Patients in whom the corpus callosum has been severed can still function in society. However, they have difficulty in connecting language and thoughts, words and pictures, and making common associations that you and I likely take for granted.

On the average, the callosum connection is thicker in women, with 20 million more fibers than in men. This allows each hemisphere to exchange information more freely. While each side of the brain does process things differently, some of our earlier assumptions about the left-right brain split are outdated now.

In general, the brain's left hemisphere processes information more sequentially. Musicians commonly process music in their left hemisphere, though a novice would probably process it in the right. Among left-handers, almost half of them use their right hemisphere for language. Higher-level mathematicians, problem-solvers and chess players have more right hemisphere activation, while beginners in those activities usually are left-hemisphere active. Gross motor function is controlled by the right hemisphere while fine motor is usually more left hemisphere activity. The right hemisphere recognizes negative emotions faster. The left hemisphere notices positive ones faster. Studies indicate that the left hemisphere is more active when we are experiencing positive emotions.

Sometimes the hemisphere we use changes over time. For example, in infants, some of the earliest language processing is right hemisphere, then by age three and four, it has moved to the left hemisphere. Females tend to develop their left hemisphere earlier than males. This gives them a distinct advantage in language and reading skills. Males are superior to females in right hemisphere development at age five, but both sexes even out by age eight or nine. Males tend to become more right hemisphere as they grow past age fifty into their older years.

Suffice it to say that the old biases about music and arts being "right brained frills" are outdated. The old reductionist models, the ones that tend to want to locate every thought and behavior in a specific place in the brain, still adhere to the left-right brain model. But many of today's top thinkers consider anything that happens in the brain as happening throughout the entire body system.

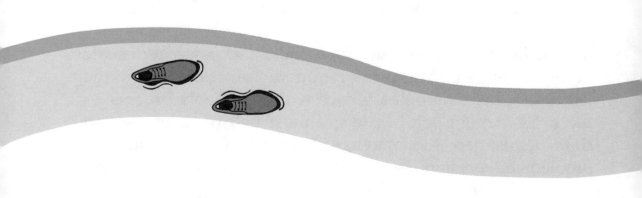

The middle or "medial brain" is the region be~~~~ frontal lobes and in front of the occipital lobe. T~~~ ~erm represents a *geographical* location. The commonly used expression "limbic brain," refers also to the mid-brain area, bit it represents a *functional* location in the brain. It defines the part of the brain that processes our emotions. Some researchers believe that we do not have a "limbic system," only specific pathways upon which our emotions travel. Much of the middle of the brain area is *not* involved in processing emotions. That's the role of our peptides floating throughout the body. Here is a description of some of the key structures located in the medial-brain:

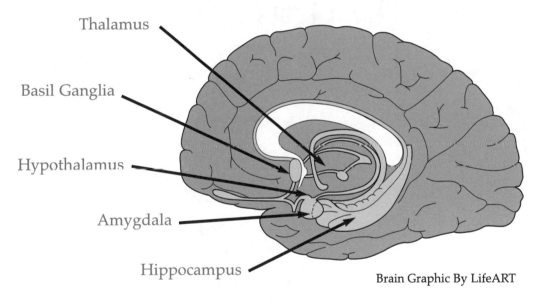

Thalamus
Basil Ganglia
Hypothalamus
Amygdala
Hippocampus

Brain Graphic By LifeART

Thalamus
The sorting station for most sensory input.

Hypothalamus
Located below the thalamus; it's the brain's thermostat regulating body functions. Operates on feedback.

Basil Ganglia
An important area responsible for motor functions.

Amygdala

An almond-shaped structure located low in the middle of the brain. It processes intense emotions.

Hippocampus

A crescent-shaped structure curving from the top to the bottom of the middle of the brain. It's responsible for the formation of explicit long-term memories.

The Brain Stem

Includes the Pons which regulates facial sensations and movements; and the Medulla which regulates and relays many nonconscious operations like heartbeat, breathing, and digestion.

Cerebellum:
"The Little Brain"

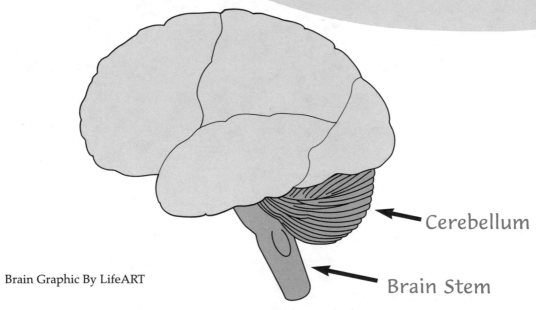

← Cerebellum

Brain Graphic By LifeART

← Brain Stem

Located near the brain stem, below the occipital lobe, the cerebellum (or "Little Brain") is involved in posture, coordination, balance, motor memory, plus novelty learning, and other cognitive activities.

The cerebellum, an area most commonly linked to movement, turns out to be a virtual switchboard of cognitive activity. The cerebellum takes up just one-tenth of the brain by volume, but contains over half of all the brain's total neurons. It has some 40 million nerve fibers, 40 times more than even the highly complex optical tract. These fibers not only feed information from the cortex to the cerebellum, but they feed them back to the cortex. If the cerebellum were only for motor function (as was once thought), why would the connections be so powerfully distributed in both directions to all areas of the brain? This subsection of the brain, long known for its role in posture, balance and movement may be our brain's sleeping giant.

Evidence of the linkage between mind and body began decades ago when Henrietta and Alan Leiner, two Stanford University neuroscientists, began research that was to eventually redraw "the cognitive map." They made some critical discoveries that spurred years of fruitful research. As an example, the cerebellum was thought to merely process signals from the cerebrum and send them to the motor cortex. But, "The mistake," say the Leiners, "was in assuming the signals went only to the motor cortex. They don't." The last place information is processed in the cerebellum, before it is sent to the cortex, is the dentate nucleus. This tiny portion of the brain is non-existent in most mammals, yet it is largest in primates which also have the highest learning capabilities. An even smaller area, the neodentate nucleus, is present only in humans and may play a significant role in thinking and a critical role in learning. The mind-body, cognitive-movement relationship underscores the importance of an enriched curriculum.

Brain Challenge

Draw a medial (side) view of the brain in the space below:

Brain "Cell"ebration:
Far-out Facts About Brain Cells

There are two kinds of brain cells: Neurons and Glia. Though the majority of brain cells (85 percent) are glia, it is the remaining 15 percent - the neurons - that give you your brain power. A huge amount of the brain's information transfer happens through the cell-to-cell process. When stimulated, brain cells grow branch-like extensions called dendrites. Each cell has one extending "leg" called an axon. The axons can grow up to a meter long. They often subdivide many times. Only axons connect with dendrites; dendrites don't connect with other dendrites.

Neurons will typically make 1,000 to 50,000 connections with other neurons. We are born with more connections than we'll need, but we lose about half of our brain's connections by age 12. A typical brain has well over a trillion connections.

1. New research suggests we can and do grow new brain cells or neurons (Reference: April 3, 1997 Nature Magazine). The research team was led by Fred Gage at Salk Institute of Biological Studies in San Diego.

2. Neurons don't sleep. A normal functioning neuron is continuously firing, integrating and generating information; it's a virtual hotbed of activity.

3. No neuron is an end point or termination for information-- it only serves to pass it on. All electrical activity in the brain travels from the neural body down the axon.

4. A single neuron may connect through its dendrites with 1,000 to 50,000 other cells. That's a good sign; the more the connections your cells make, the better. How many connections a

neuron makes with other connections is determined by genes, enrichment, and its specific location. Cells in the cerebellum have the greatest dendritic branching.

5. The sum total of all the synaptic reactions arriving from all the dendrites to the cell body at any moment will determine whether that cell will, in fact, fire. It needs a "majority vote." In other words, learning is the critical function of neurons that cannot be accomplished individually--it requires groups of neurons.

6. Most adult neurons stay put; they simply extend an axon outward. While many fibers (dendrites) may extend from a neuron, each neuron has only one axon. An axon is a thinner, leg-like extension that connects to dendrites.

7. The axon has two essential functions: to conduct information in the form of electrical stimulation and to transport chemical substances. The longest ones may be up to a meter long. The thicker the axons, the faster it conducts electricity (and information).

8. Myelin is a lipid (fatty) substance that forms around well-used axons. The most used neurons are myelinated. This seems not only to speed up the electrical transmission (up to twelve-fold), but also to reduce interference from other nearby reactions.

9. The point of contact between two neurons is the synapse. It's a micro gap where the electrical nerve impulse traveling down the axon triggers the release of chemical messengers (neurotransmitters) stored at the end of the axon. They are absorbed by the receptor sites in the connecting dendrites.

10. The synapse is the point of communication for less than two percent of the body's total communication. The rest of it comes from the floating information bundles known as peptides that lock into receptor sites and transfer data through absorption.

Learning Happens...
But How?

Scientists are unsure exactly how humans learn, but they have some ideas about what happens in the process.

A Stimulus to the Brain Starts the Process

It could be internal (a brainstorm!) or it could be a new experience, like solving a jigsaw puzzle. Novel mental or motor stimulation produces beneficial electrical energy that helps stimulate neural growth.

Processing Stimuli at a Neuronal Level

The prevailing theory states learning is electro-chemical in nature. Electrical energy generated by our senses normally travels to extraction and sorting stations like the thalamus located in the middle of the brain area. From there, electrical signals are sent to various areas of the brain. When the cell body stimulates the axon with electrical energy, it stimulates the release of those stored chemicals into the synaptic gap (the space between the end of an axon and tip of a dendrite).

Formation of a Memory Potential

A gene is responsible for activating the formation of long-term memory. It's activates a switch known as CREB which signals the neuron to activate either short- or long-term memory. If a weaker stimulus is then applied to the neighboring cell some time later, the cell's ability to get excited is enhanced.

In other words, cells change their receptivity to messages based on previous stimulation. This lasting learning or LTP (long-term potentiation) is tentatively accepted by most scientists as the physical process that stores learning.

Are Today's Kids Different?

Change in Diet

Today, kids maintain a higher fat, sugar, and carbohydrates diet. Foods impact the functioning, but not the structure, of the brain. However, excessive alcohol destroys tissue.

Drug and Medication Usage

Blurred lines exist between drugs and medications. More kids are willing to take something to alter mind and body states. Long-term effects on the brain are unknown.

Less "Crawl-Time" and Physical Activity

Poor motor development is being impacted by an increase in the amount of inactive time spent in automobiles, watching television, and in front of computers; the disappearance of swings, see-saws, and merry-go-rounds; a reduction in school physical education programs; and a lack of emphasis on walking or riding bikes versus motorized transportation.

Social/Economic Stability

Many children are growing up with fewer resources. In 1960, 90 percent of all unwed mothers gave up their baby for adoption to qualified families. Today, over 90 percent of all unwed mothers keep their babies, in spite of a lack of financial, health, or emotional resources.

School Budget Cuts

Fewer music, drama, and arts classes are available in public schools today. As resources tighten, the arts are often considered a "right-brained frill." Many decision-makers know better, but not all; and in the midst of competing agendas, the arts are wrongly considered unessential.

Threat, Stress and Violence

More kids are impacted by excess violence on television; and by violence in their homes, schools, and communities.

More Hours of Television Per Week

The average child is watching television two to five hours per day (20-30 hours per week). Excessive television viewing leads to greater passivity and less thinking time. Too many kids are learning about the world second hand! Some concern exists regarding the impact of TV on the developmental stages of children. It is best to have children refrain from viewing before the age of seven; and to monitor their viewing time after that. Scientists are considering that flat-screen technology may impair eye development; and we're not sure yet how the brain deals with abstract violence at various stages of development. Time would be better spent doing more physical activities.

Boy's and Girl's Brains:
Genetic Differences

The descriptions below indicate what neuroscientists typically call a female or male brain. Keep in mind that they are based on statistical averages; and that in real life variance in hormone levels, behaviors, and brain structure exists.

Female Brain

- The left hemisphere develops earlier than the right.
- Has a larger corpus callosum (3 to 10 percent more fibers) than male.

- Has monthly fluctuations in hormones, progesterone, and estrogen which cause shifting scores on spatial, math, verbal, and fine motor skills tests (lower hormone levels result in a boost in scores on spatial and math tests; higher hormone levels result in a boost in verbal and fine motor skills).
- Has 20 to 30 percent more serotonin which is linked to fearfullness, shyness, low self-confidence, obsessive-compulsive behavior, and unduly dampened aggression.
- Spreads thinking function over a wider area of the brain which translates to fewer learning disabilities.
- Hypothalamus uses positive internal feedback which maximizes hormonal fluctuations.

Male Brain

- The right hemisphere develops earlier than in females which impacts classroom discipline and preferences in sports.
- Moderate testosterone level aids skill in abstract manipulation, spatial, science, math, sports, business, computers, etc.
- Is more compartmentalized in usage than in female due to narrower corpus callosum.
- Has 20 to 30 percent less serotonin. This level is linked to impulsive aggression, suicide, alcoholism, depression, impulsive aggression, and explosive rage.
- Hypothalamus uses negative internal feedback which minimizes hormonal fluctuations.
- Testosterone linked to aggression and competitiveness also increases behavior preservation.

Trail Journal

_____

_____

_____

_____

_____

_____

_____

_____

_____

_____

_____

_____

_____

_____

_____

_____

_____

Learning Disabilities:
The Giant Soup Bowl

Though learning conditions are often lumped into one large soup bowl called "disabilities," each student needs to be carefully and independently diagnosed. An accurate diagnosis will lead to an effective response and treatment.

Reading Problems...

Are sometimes the result of the brain just not being ready to read. Or functions such as faulty sentence construction, noun-pronoun switching, grammar, and phonological switches can be the result of neural disorders caused by various conditions including stressful pregnancies, emotional or physical trauma, or lack of an enriched early childhood environment.

Attention Deficit Disorder...

Has become a catch-word for a variety of behaviors which can be the result of genetic predisposition, compromised neural pathways, or neurotransmitter (serotonin/dopamine) irregularities. Symptoms include prolonged fidgeting, restlessness, impulsiveness, etc. Drug intervention ought to be a last resort. Other interventions like a change of diet, class level, teachers, or teaching strategies should be made first.

Dyslexia...

Is likely caused by even hemispheric development or early hearing problems. It may be correlated to inappropriate hormone levels. Clearly defined cases are usually treatable. New software is available for therapeutic intervention.

Tourette's...

Occurs more in males and begins between 2 and 12 years of age. Symptoms include inattention and involuntary sounds and motions. Treatment is usually the medication Haldol.

On the Fast Track to:
Understanding Neurotransmitters

Neurotransmitters...

Are our brain's biochemical messengers. We have about 50 of them. These are the stimulus or the inhibitors that regulate neural activity.

Acetylcholine...

Is a common neurotransmitter, particularly involved in long-term memory formation. Specifically released at neuromuscular junctions, it's present at higher levels during sleep.

Dopamine...

Is a powerful and common neurotransmitter primarily involved in producing a positive mood or feelings. Secreted by neurons in the substantia nigra, mid-brain and hypothalamus, it plays a role in movements, too. Dopamine deficits are found in patients suffering from Parkinson's Disease.

GABA...

Or gamma-aminobutyric acid, is a neurotransmitter that acts as an inhibitory agent - an "off" switch in the brain.

Serotonin...

Is a common neurotransmitter, most responsible for inducing relaxation, and regulating mood and sleep. It's the "brakes" in our brain, modulating our urges. Males average about 20 to 30 percent less than females. Antidepressants (like Prozac) usually suppress the absorption of serotonin which affects learning, attention, sleep, arousal, and memory. Serotonin is generally excitatory - just the right amount is good, too much makes us fearful, lacking self-confidence and obsessive-compulsive. Too little makes us aggressive, violent, and sometimes deviant.

When Our Brain Fails Us

Brain Aging

Causes: Humans don't usually die of old age. We get diseases, organs break down, we have accidents, mineral deficiencies, or we lose the will to live.

Treatment: Stay physically active--neurons need oxygen from a fresh, rich blood supply. Go for walks and maintain a fitness program. Seek novel challenges with frequent problem solving. Resting the brain is the quickest way to wear it out. Eat carefully, avoid toxins, and get your trace minerals - especially selenium, copper, and boron.

Parkinson's Disease

Causes: Atrophy of nerve cells in the mid-brain area (the substantia nigra cells in the basal ganglia) which causes a decrease in the release of the neurotransmitter dopamine. Some speculate environmental toxins play a part.

Affects: 1 in 200; affects more men than women and more non-smokers than smokers.

Symptoms: Muscle tremor, motor deficits, memory loss.

Treatment: No known cure, only dopamine supplements like L-Dopa.

Alzheimer's

Causes: Linked to a gene disorder (located on chromosome #21); not contagious, no clear causes, runs in families; also linked to toxins, lack of intellectual stimulation.

Affects: 1 in 10; usually begins in 60's; lasts 3 to 15 years before death.

Symptoms: Memory loss is first; later symptoms are poor judgment, mood changes, loss of mental ability, and helplessness.

Treatment: Estrogen seems to prevent it, new drugs delay symptoms (i.e., Cognex-Tacrine, Hyperzine and Aricept).

REST STOP

Reflection and Processing Time...

What did you just learn about the brain? What meaning does it have for you?

Trail Guide to Applications:
Section 2

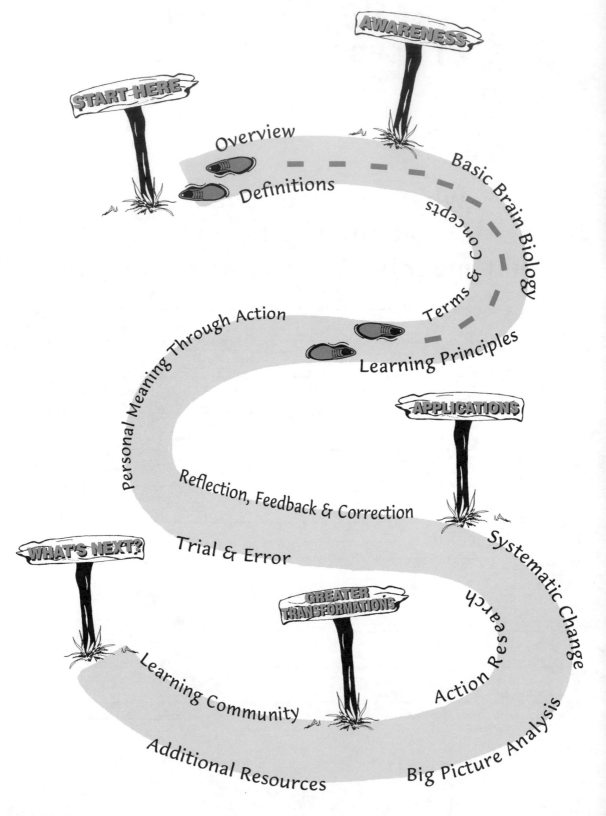

START HERE

AWARENESS

Overview

Definitions

Basic Brain Biology

Terms & Concepts

Personal Meaning Through Action

Learning Principles

APPLICATIONS

Reflection, Feedback & Correction

WHAT'S NEXT?

Trial & Error

Systematic Change

GREATER TRANSFORMATIONS

Action Research

Learning Community

Big Picture Analysis

Additional Resources

Brain-Compatible Learning:
Recipe Not Required

Remember, brain-compatible learning theory is not a doctrine, nor is it a recipe to follow.

Brain-compatible learning is, rather, a comprehensive approach to learning based on how the brain learns best. And since the human brain is unique, there is no "one best" way to do it. What you'll want to know (and embody) are the *principles* of how the brain works. When your work is true to the principles, you'll be using a brain-compatible approach.

In no particular order, the following represent the most important principles:

Key Principles of
Brain-Compatible Learning

Uniqueness

Every single brain is totally unique.

How does your instruction and assessment reflect this principle?

Impact of High Stress or Threat

Since the brain's priority is always survival, threat throws the brain into survival mode at the expense of developing higher order thinking skills.

Can you identify the five most common sources of stress or threat in homes and schools? Do you have a plan to systematically deal with these stresses that alter and impair learning and even kill brain cells?

Developmental Stages of Readiness

Developmental stages vary in children. Typically a three-year span of variance is considered normal.

What are some examples of how you are understanding and using the stages of readiness?

The Nature of Enrichment

The brain can grow new connections at any age.
Complex, challenging experiences with feedback are best.
Cognitive skills develop better with music and motor skills.

Are you planning each lesson with enrichment in mind? How so?

Emotions Critical to Learning

Emotions drive our attention, health, learning, meaning, memory, and survival.

How are they acknowledged and embedded in the learning and social process? What are the specific ways you consistently allow for emotional expression?

Memory and Retrieval Pathways

Information and experiences are stored in a variety of pathways.

Do you know what these pathways are; and how do you ensure they're used? Do you incorporate physical activity daily in the classroom?

All Learning Is Mind-Body

Movement, foods, attention cycles, drugs, and chemicals all have a powerful modulating effect on learning.

What percentage of learning is done at the student's seat versus through activities?

Patterns and Programs Drive Our Understanding
Intelligence is the ability to elicit and to construct useful patterns.

How do you deal with this reality in a practical way?

The Brain Is Meaning-Driven
Meaning is more important to the brain than information.

In what ways do you purposely set out to help ensure meaning-making?

Rich, Nonconscious Learning
We process both parts and wholes simultaneously; and we are affected by a great deal of peripheral influences.

How is this reality addressed in your learning environment, instructional practices, and curriculum?

The Social Brain
Intelligence is valued in the context of the society we live in.

The brain develops better in concert with others; how do you use this principle?

Complex and Adaptive System
Every brain adapts to its environment based on experience. Effective change involves the entire complex system.

In what ways do you address a systematic approach, not just the content of learning?

Footnote: Acknowledgements to Geoffrey and Renate Caine for the development of the principles listed above.

Oops.....

Those are a mouthful!
Go back and re-read them.
Now, it's processing time....
How is your own work reflected in
these principles?

_____

_____

_____

_____

_____

_____

_____

_____

REST STOP

Now that you've reread the principles, let's
explore them in a bit more detail.

Principle #1:
Uniqueness

Every single brain is totally unique.

How does your instruction and assessment reflect this principle?

As different as a fingerprint, your brain differs, as well, from any other on earth. Even the brains of identical twins are different. How did they become so? Is it just the "software" (environmental influences) or the "hardware" (genetic influences), too?

It's both! Surprisingly, not only is the hard-wiring of the nervous system very customized, but so is the "soft-wiring" of the personality, the character, the learning styles, and emotional system.

- Every brain is given a different blueprint through DNA at birth.
- Every brain physically changes its wiring through its experiences.
- Some brains have adapted to better recognize emotions.
- Some children have spent more time at counting and math.
- Some have gotten good at working under stress.
- Some may be quite musical.

The point is, therefore, that comparison among learners is not only pointless, it falsely assumes that learners are dealing with the same "hardware." They are not. A brain which has physically rewired itself in adaptation to its uniquely personal experiences, learns in its own way.

Even hormone levels are unique to each individual. This is why the whole notion of states, learning styles, moods, personalized learning, choice, mastery learning, personality inventories and multiple intelligences makes sense.

This principal suggests we ought to avoid grade-level comparisons, gender comparisons, age, school, or district-by-district comparisons. All that makes sense is comparing one student to him or herself at a later time.

Principle #2:
Impact of Threat or High Stress

The brain's priority is always survival. Threat throws the brain into survival mode at the expense of developing higher order thinking skills.

Can you identify the five most common sources of stress in the home and school? Do you have a plan to systematically deal with these stresses that alter and impair learning and kill brain cells?

We used to think that threatening students was just bad teaching. Now, we know that it impairs brain cells. Threat also changes the body's chemistry and impacts learning. If you do nothing else, learn to recognize the sources of threat and high stress in your classroom. Then, take purposeful and continuous steps to eradicate them.

Examples of threat include anything that embarrasses students, unrealistic deadlines, a student's inability to speak a language, uncomfortable classroom cultures, a bully in the hallway, inappropriate learning styles, and out of class things that may include anything from bad traffic to a fight with a family member. A little to moderate amount of stress is good for learning. Lasting high stress (weeks or more) or threat is deadly. It reduces our brain's capacity for understanding, meaning, memory, and developing higher order thinking skills.

This principle suggests we ought to be very careful to keep high stress and threat out of the learning environment. We ought to preface each learning experience with a relaxation exercise , when appropriate, that allows students to process or express pent-up emotions.

Trail Journal

_____

_____

_____

_____

_____

_____

Check It Out

Let's personalize what you have just read about stress by identifying your own behaviors. Check off those you've used in the last 30 days.

1. Did you tell a student that if he or she did something, they would have to go to the principal's office?
   Probably _____ Yes _____ No_____

2. Did you ask a question of the class that you already knew the right answer to?
   Probably _____ Yes _____ No_____

3. Did you suggest to the class that if they were "good" they might get out early?
   Probably _____ Yes _____ No_____

4. Did you use any "caught you being good" stickers or certificates?
   Probably _____ Yes _____ No_____

5. Did you let students know that if they were unruly, they may have to stay late?
   Probably _____ Yes _____ No_____

6. Did you call on a student to respond to a question who did not volunteer to be called on?
   Probably _____ Yes _____ No_____

7. Did you use any kind of rewards to get better behaviors?
   Probably _____ Yes _____ No_____

8. Is there some kind of a scorecard or public listing of student misbehaviors posted in your class?
   Probably _____ Yes _____ No_____

9. Do you start your class with content like, "Please open your books to page 21?" Or, "Everyone please find your home work and get ready to hand it in."
   Probably _____ Yes _____ No_____

10. Did you compare any individual students to others or tell any individual student that "You're not living up to your potential."
    Probably _____ Yes _____ No_____

The first place to start is with awareness. Most stressful classes and threatening events are not perceived as such by the teacher. If you answered "Yes" to any of the preceding questions, then you are very likely creating states of high stress or threat. Students get stressed by comparisons, threats, rewards, or even classes that start with content, not people. Learn to put how kids feel first, then move to the content afterwards.

Principle #3: Developmental Stages of Readiness

Developmental stages vary in children. Typically a three-year-span of variance is considered normal.

What are some examples of how you are understanding and using the stages of readiness?

General, though not hard and fast, "windows" for learning do exist. Every window provides a unique opportunity; once the window of opportunity passes, the learning process changes. Some windows of learning to be aware of are:

Language
Genetic: we are born with the structure for grammar.
- Birth to 12 months: we learn the sounds (and accent) of our native language.
- One to ten years: we learn the generic vocabulary and emotional phrasing. This is the best time for foreign language learning.
- 10+ years: Best time for complex patterns, grammar, spelling, specialized vocabularies.

Math and Logic
Genetic: we are born with the basic knowledge of counting and physics.

- Birth to 3 years: we learn the physical properties of the world.
- 3 to 10 years: we learn the vocabulary, the simple and the fine motor movements.
- 10+ years: Best time for more complex patterns.

Emotional Intelligence
Genetic: we are born with a propensity for a certain emotional temperament.

- Birth to 24 months: we learn the proper feeling-responses that are appropriate for our family and culture.
- 2 to 15 years: we learn the socialized community response.
- 15+ years: we learn new emotional responses much more slowly.

Music
Genetic: we are born with the receptivity for and ability to hear music.

- Birth to 36 months: we learn the key sounds, songs, and voices of our native culture.
- 1 to 10 years: this is the best time to learn to play an instrument, to appreciate music, and for singing.
- 10+ years: best time to learn the technical nature of music and more complex music.

*This principle suggests that we might reorganize **when** we do things to maximize the brain's capacity to learn them. For example, learning a new language or musical instrument should be a K-5 activity, rather than one delayed for the later years.*

REST STOP

Reflection Time...

Can you personalize what you just read?
How do the previous principles impact you?

Principle #4:
The Nature of Enrichment

The brain can grow new connections at any age. Complex, challenging experiences with feedback are best. Cognitive skills develop better with music and motor skills.

Are you planning each day with enrichment in mind? How so?

The Brain Physically Changes in Three Ways:

1. ### Genetic:
   ### Intrinsic Forces Change Us
   Also known as nature or "pre-wiring."
   - There's a hierarchy of automated species-specific cell behaviors.
   - Some structures are genetic, others triggered by prenatal conditions.
   - Patterns (not single-point, individual cell mutations) are what's causal. This means one cell is nearly irrelevant, but clusters and patterns of them are important.
   - It's the regulatory process, not individual genes that do it.

2. ### Synaptic Overproduction:
   ### Our Brain Prepares Us
   Also known as "experience expectant" processes. Your brain expects something important to happen.
   - This is massive overproduction of synapses prior to demand.

48

- Later, it's followed by their selective elimination (or preservation). This "pruning" eliminates up to half of your synapses by age 15.
- Process is highly space-competitive so what space is not used by one activity may be taken up by others.
- Researchers think the process may be "sensory specific" early on and "cognitive specific" later on. Your brain prioritizes space for all sensory enrichment early, but shifts priorities after ages 10 to 20 for thinking.

3. Experience Dependent: We Respond to Our Environment

Also known as "experience dependent" processes. This is what we commonly used to talk about as enrichment.

- But the experiences must be coherent and novel to the brain.
- They also must be uncontaminated with reliable cause and effect.
- New research says that the brain can produce new cells and this means there's always hope for the brain.

Ultimately...
It's Nature _and_ Nurture

In numbers one to three above, the processes are separated. Yet such separations are not so clear in a developing brain. Rather there's a give-and-take, push-and-pull development process. Researchers are still unsure of all the triggers for cell growth. We are unsure of all the mechanisms. We do know, however, that there's an almost magical interplay that helps the brain adapt and grow. Thank goodness we can always update our brain.

Smart Rats:
Effects of Enriched Environments on Brain Structure in Rats

In studies on rats, the following environments were examined to determine effects of enrichment. The environments below are listed from *most* to *least* effective:

 Complex (play-exploration, animal and object-filled): This condition resulted in the smartest rats.

 Social (families, mother with pups): Family support helped, but was not everything.

 Isolated (no toys, no friends): This was the worst condition and produced the least curious rats.

In Other Experiments...

 Acrobatic Learning (required challenges): Here rats had to leap from elevated platforms for food.

 Exercise (treadmills, very little new learning): They all had increased blood flow.

 Choice Exercise (choice, free access): Exercisers had increased blood flow, others did not.

 Inactivity (standard cages): These rats, with the least enrichment, did the worst.

What conclusions can you draw about the possible implications for your classroom and enrichment?

Enriched Diets:
Ingredients of a Brain-Smart Classroom

The brain does have "elastic" qualities. It changes physically depending on experience. The effects of enrichment may include more dendrites per neuron, more synapses per neuron, an increase in neural activity, an increase in tissue volume, greater density of capillaries, and greater blood flow.

The relevant feature of synaptic formation is that it must accompany learning. "Super-enriched" environments produced no better results than those from the complex or acrobatic groups.

Research tells us the brain continues to "re-wire" itself with the production of synapses through our life. Synapses are the junction points between two brain cells. The more you learn, the more you physically change your brain. For decades it was thought that the brain did not generate new cells. The newest research suggests that the brain does grow new cells with proper stimulation (at least in the hippocampus, an area responsible for memory). This means there's still enormous potential in all of us for lifelong learning.

Enrichment does not guarantee a better citizen in society. It merely lays down the neural forests for optimal intelligence. Instilling productive and healthy social and moral values is much more complicated; it is influenced by many variables including the family, church, individual, community, and the school.

Enriched classrooms are *not* those with mobiles, posters, fish tanks, and pets. There is, however, nothing wrong with these at all. But never confuse these items with the things that physically alter the structure of the brain and foster genuine enrichment: novelty, challenge, and feedback.

Challenge and Feedback:
Critical Ingredients

Enrichment comes primarily from challenge and feedback. But what about the teacher who seemed to do a good job the "traditional way?" The old days of "stand and deliver" are not only out of date, they represent bad teaching. Teachers who think of themselves as star performers usually leave drained at the end of each day's performance. Just as sad are the teachers frozen in a time warp who still believe that their job is to convey information. Schools can't compete with television, phones, and computers in the information age. Today's teachers must think of themselves as a catalyst for learning, not a live, breathing textbook. Schools simply must have greater roles, like creating motivated, thinking, responsible, and productive citizens for the next century.

Enrichment now takes on another dimension: What kinds of enrichment will make for tomorrow's better citizens? Here's a clue: music training should be a part of every child's education. Not because music appreciation cultivates broader cultural horizons, but because the evidence suggests that music is a brain-building block for math and science. Art may be valuable for building emotional intelligence. Dance may increase cognitive skills. We are learning much now about the positive impact of the arts on the young learner.

We ought to engage the arts as part of every subject. Music belongs in your classes, as does drawing and theater.

How else might you use music, theater, dance, and art?

_____

_____

Challenge...

Stimulates brain growth:
Too little means boredom,
Too much can intimidate

Examples of Challenge:

Relevant problem-solving
Competitive/Cooperative games
Writing, arts, drama
Complex projects

Tools to Create Challenge:

Vary time allotted
Change circumstances
Vary resources available
Alter standards of quality

Example:

A simple activity like creating a safety book becomes very challenging if you reduce the time allowed, ask students to work alone instead of with partners or a small team, prevent them from using computers or make the standard so high that it creates hopelessness. Or, if orchestrated well, it can be the perfect activity that engages students, is fun, and fills them with meaning.

Feedback...

Is Usually:
Too Little,
Too Late,
Too Vague;
Presented in the Wrong Form, and
Therefore, Lacks Impact

The brain is designed to survive and thrive by learning and getting feedback. Feedback is the second of the two key ingredients for optimal enrichment. Yet, most students are starved for both quality and quantity of feedback. The best feedback is specific, student-controlled, and sometimes dramatic.

Starvation Is Bad...

The reason most students are starved for feedback is simple: most teachers think of themselves as the primary source of feedback. But teachers don't have enough time each day to be the *one* to give the specific feedback that every learner needs to have.

Students who lack sufficient feedback (at least once every 30 minutes) will either go out of their way to get attention (pester the teacher or be a discipline problem) or, they'll simply lose interest in the class and "check out." Disinterested and disengagment in the classroom is a common complaint among teachers.

The solution is simple: teachers should be the secondary source of feedback, not the primary source. Get out of the way and let kids get the feedback they need. There are countless ways to provide more feedback to your learners; The following suggestions represent the tip of the iceberg:

Feedback Suggestions

- __ Computers
- __ Peer editing
- __ Show and tell
- __ Suggestion box
- __ Multi-age teaching
- __ journal feedback
- __ Student goals
- __ Rubrics
- __ Agreed upon standards
- __ Parents comment
- __ Learning log
- __ Community projects
- __ Group evaluations
- __ Small group presentations
- __ Rituals of greeting
- __ Pair share
- __ Class/school yellow pages
- __ Peer correcting
- __ Checklist
- __ Listing of information on walls
- __ Other teacher's feedback
- __ Timeline
- __ Student predictions
- __ Other classes give feedback

With maximum feedback, you'll get maximum brain enrichment. This is the core strategy of a brain-compatible classroom. Remove threat and enrich like crazy. By doing this, you can expect miracles.

This principle suggest that we ought to never give up on a learner. The brain is always capable of learning something new.

Your new teaching commitments:

_____

_____

Principle #5:
Emotions Essential to Learning

Emotions drive our attention, health, learning, meaning, memory, and survival.

How are they acknowledged and embedded in the learning and social processes? What are the specific ways you consistently allow for emotional expression?

How the Chemical-Emotional Brain Connection Works

One way our brain and body communicates is via cell-to-cell stimulation. One cell talks to another, creating or utilizing synapses formed by electrical-to-chemical-to-electrical stimulation. This is only one of the brain's two information-processing systems. Surprisingly, it is the least efficient and smaller of the two!

The largest percent of communication within the brain and body is carried out by a simple, but powerful process that happens millions of times per second. Each of our neurons has on its surface opiate receptors. Cells typically have several million receptors of about 70 different varieties. The receptor is a single molecule composed of proteins in the form of stranded amino acids. These receptors function as sensing molecules, hovering in the cell membranes, waiting for the right chemicals to swim up to them and bind.

When this binding occurs, it's a bit like a lock and key arrangement. The chemical key - the agitator - is called a ligand. Using a more common metaphor, the receptor sites and ligands act as if they are having molecular sex (see figure below). Ligands can be the common neurotransmitters called steroids which include hormones, but 95 percent of the time, they're peptides.

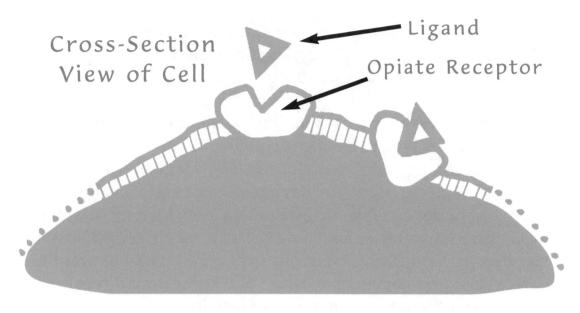

Opiate Receptor Receiving
(or Communicating With) Ligand

Peptides, which are strings of amino acids like receptors, are distributed throughout the body and brain. They travel in the bloodstream, unencumbered by the brain's fixed axonal and dendritic highway system. Peptides are the brain and body's primary source of information transfer, responsible for as much as 98 percent of all communications. In short, peptides are the body's second nervous system.

This new understanding helps us to piece together several experiences. Have you ever had a "gut feeling" about something? Or felt that you knew something on an unconscious level, but couldn't explain it? Peptides, busy processing information, are present in your gastrointestinal lining. The body is the unconscious mind! This systems-level approach explains how the entire body contains and transfers information. Another way of looking at it is, our entire body thinks, not just our brain.

Moods and Optimal States

Moods and states are created and circulated throughout the body by peptides. Peptides carry over 98 percent of all internal information.

While excessive emotions can impair rational thinking, the absence of emotion and feeling is equally damaging to the functions of reasoning and rationality. The old adage of keeping the class's emotions in check, or "having an even keel," is outdated. Positive emotions create an excitement and love of learning. They spur motivation to learn and tell us if we are confident. On the other hand, negative emotions unchecked make us want to leave a class and never come back. Or, if orchestrated sensitively, they can generate a lasting love of learning.

This principle suggests we ought to purposely engage learners with circumstances, projects, and ideas which elicit productive emotions. Examples include: use of celebrations, storytelling, curiosity, competition, mystery, big projects, drama, physical activity, and music.

What strategies to evoke emotions are you using currently? Are there others you would like to implement?

_____

_____

_____

Wait!

There are big-time implications to the discoveries on the previous page.
Can you guess what they are?
Hey, it's okay to speculate...

REST STOP

Principle #6:
Memory and Retrieval Pathways

Information and experiences are stored in a variety of pathways. Do you know what these pathways are? How do you ensure they're used?

Our brain does not store memories, it recreates them, very approximately, every time we recall. We don't have "memory banks." Rather we have pathways for specific types of learning. Some pathways are more easily retrieved than others. For example, textbook and other forms of rote learning create significant difficulties for students. Retrieval is better in contextual, episodic, event-oriented situations; or by using motor learning, location changes, music, and rhythm. Use of multiple strategies works best followed by daily and weekly review. Learn what the pathways are and how to use them.

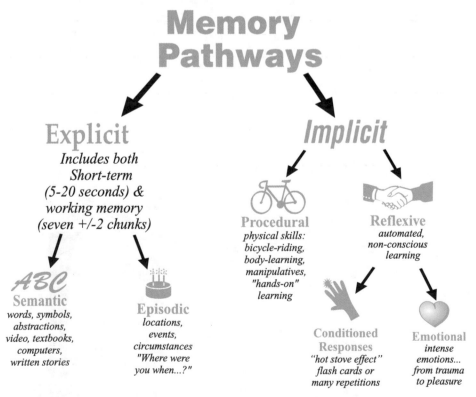

Memory Pathways

Explicit
Includes both Short-term (5-20 seconds) & working memory (seven +/-2 chunks)

ABC
Semantic
words, symbols, abstractions, video, textbooks, computers, written stories

Episodic
locations, events, circumstances "Where were you when...?"

Implicit

Procedural
physical skills: bicycle-riding, body-learning, manipulatives, "hands-on" learning

Reflexive
automated, non-conscious learning

Conditioned Responses
"hot stove effect" flash cards or many repetitions

Emotional
intense emotions... from trauma to pleasure

60

Maximizing Multiple Memory Pathways

Rule 1:   *Never assume that because your students don't recall information easily that they don't know it. It may be stored in a different pathway.*

Rule 2:   *For maximum recall, store learning in multiple pathways AND follow up with review 10 minutes, 2 days, and 1 week later.*

How We Retrieve Our Memories:

Semantic

- Teach students how to make and use acronyms, key words, peg words, word associations, and mnemonics. Remind them that all reading must be processed as it's read by mapping, journaling, or discussion. Encourage students to create multiple categories and groupings for their learning.

Episodic

- Allow students to learn standing up, sitting on the floor, or sitting on the desk. Prepare lessons that take the class outside, in the cafeteria, or on a field-trip. Bring in guest speakers, change the lighting, let kids wear costumes, etc. Remember the movie "Dead Poet's Society"? Experiences that engage your students' imaginations and emotions, and are novel in character and location will be "ascribed" a special memory "address" in the brain that will be easier to recall.

Procedural

- Ensure that students get to move as a way to embed learning. Engage motion, hands-on learning, manipulatives, stretch breaks, drama, theater, and role-play.

Reflexive

- Students can learn through the productive engagement of strong emotions, as well as with flashcard-type learning that becomes automated with repetition.

In summary to maximize memory, engage emotions, and provide variety, repetition, and movement.

This principle suggests that we ought to actively pursue the use of multiple storage and retrieval pathways to optimize learning activation.

What are some strategies you would like to try to help students maximize memory retrieval?

_____

_____

_____

_____

_____

_____

Principle #7:
Learning Is Mind-Body Integrated

Movement, foods, attention cycles, drugs, and chemicals have a powerful modulating effect on learning.

What percentage of learning is done at the student's seat versus through activities? How do you incorporate physical activity in the classroom?

We learn as a single, integrated organism. Mind, soul, feelings, brain, arms and legs. To our brain, everything is one complex, adaptive system which creates and controls information. All learning is dependent on the body's physiological state. Correspondingly, each posture and movement stores a separate library of learning. Here are some physical (body) conditions that impact our cognition (thinking):

- Eye movements trigger modalities (visual, auditory and kinesthetic).
- Hunger and thirst disrupt sequential thinking.
- Feelings or strong emotions change attention and memory levels.
- Illness or disease lowers attention and memory capacity.
- Fluctuations in heart, pulse, and breathing rates impact learning.
- Changes (hourly, daily, and monthly) in hormones change learning.
- Stress impacts our attention and memory capacity.

The Chemistry of Behavior

Noradrenaline
Low Levels Encourage:

- Under arousal
- Thrill-seeking
- Increased tendency towards cold-blooded acts of violence

Risks of High Levels:

- Over arousal
- Temperamental
- Increased tendency towards hot-blooded acts of violence

Serotonin
Low Levels Encourage:

- Depression
- Suicide
- Alcoholism
- Explosive rage
- Deviance

Risks of High Levels:

- Shyness
- Obsessive compulsion
- Fearfulness
- Unduly dampened aggression

Moderate hormone levels allow us to function optimally. The description "low levels" above means low for that gender. A female averages 20 to 30 percent higher levels of serotonin than males. What is low for her might be high for a male. A survey of prison populations would reveal a large number of males with very low serotonin and above average noradrenaline levels. However, a variant hormone level doesn't necessarily equate to deviant behavior. It merely increases the likelihood. These general charts are merely meant to help us better understand how much behaviors are impacted by the chemicals in our bodies.

Feeding the Brain

Help your learners understand the relationship between nutrition and learning and memory. Studies confirm that a definite measurable relationship exists between what one eats and how one feels and performs. In fact, dopamine, norepinephrine, and serotonin - three chemical neurotransmitters manufactured in our brains - are constituents of the food we eat. Reacting to the foods we eat, dopamine and norepinephrine are the alertness chemicals. Serotonin is the calming chemical. Protein eaten alone or with a carbohydrate increases "brain power". On the other hand, carbohydrates eaten without protein will result in an increased sense of relaxation and focus.

There are many ways to influence the eating behaviors of kids. Talk to them about how to fix better breakfasts and pack smarter lunches. Speak about nutrition at open houses. Give parents nutritional guidelines. Role-model good eating habits. Put healthier foods in school vending machines. Work with the food service staff to prepare more nutritious meals. The human brain is 78 percent water. When dehydration occurs, attention, critical thinking, learning, and memory are impaired. Allow water bottles in your classroom or remind students to at least drink water before class to avoid dehydration.

Proper nutrition also includes sufficient protein, trace minerals, liquids, and B vitamins. We learn best with less carbohydrates and a nibbling diet. Suggest your learners read books like *Managing your Mind and Mood Through Food* by Judith Wurtman.

This principle suggests we ought to educate ourselves and our learners about the impact of various foods on cognitive ability.

Cycles and Bio-rhythms

Our brain is designed for ups and downs, not constant attention. The old notion of teachers "getting students' attention and keeping it" is outdated. Having perfect attention from a class is not only statistically improbable; it's bad for learning. Why? Down time allows our brain to "fix" neural connections, leading to better memory. Down time allows learners to construct meaning out of an experience. Much of our learning which is done on a nonconscious level, without reflection, remains on that level. You can either have your learner's attention or they can be making meaning for themselves, but not both at the same time.

Our body clocks seem to run in 90- to 110-minute cycles. These low-to-high-energy or relaxation-to-tension-cycles are called ultradian patterns. They are affected by shifts in our breathing and energy levels and dramatically affect our learning and perception of ourselves. Generally speaking, learners will focus better in the late morning and early evening; and they tend to be more pessimistic in middle to late afternoon. Physical activity or emotional engagement can modify the brain's normal rhythm. A break that incorporates physical exercise is an excellent way to alter a low cycle.

Hormones, diet, emotions, and chemistry trigger constant fluctuations in attention, memory, and learning. The terms "on" or "off" task are irrelevant to the brain. The brain is always doing what it needs to do to survive, meet challenge, or get rest. This explains why we learn better with variety and choice. Since each of us may be on different chronological, biological, and hemispheric timetables, we need room to match our most productive learning times to the tasks at hand.

This principle suggests we ought to orchestrate low- and high-energy activity levels. Gone are the days of constant direct lecture.

Attention and Learning

Here's the mind-body connection. Your body has high-low cycles of about 90 to 110 minutes. When students are at the top of these cycles, they're much more attentive. At the bottom of the cycle, energy drops and attention and learning does too. Learn to "ride with" the cycles and you'll have fewer problems. Learn to give physical breaks that are super brain energizers and you'll keep energy up, too. Here's a few other tips:

- Shorten required attention time.

- Increase choice in learning.

- Boost relevance, choice, and engagement.

- Utilize more nonconscious learning (posters, people, music, projects).

- Provide a variety of learning experiences that engage more senses.

- Use cross laterals to wake up the brain.

Optimal School Start Times

Studies suggest that as students reach the age of approximately 12 years old (until about 22 years), the body's clock modulates. The desire to go to bed later and get up later at this time appears to be biological in nature, rather than a response to peer pressure or socialization. The last couple of hours of sleep are critical to school-day attention. To maximize student alertness, learning, and memory, researchers suggest that K-5 students continue to start at the early time of 7:30am. But for students from grades 6 to 12, the morning start time ought to be closer to 9am to accommodate a teen's natural biological tendency to go to bed later and wake up later.

Elementary school
7:30am start

Middle and High school
9am start

"The Up Side of Down Time"

The brain is not designed for continuous attention. Attempting to maintain students' attention 100 percent of the time is not only bad teaching, it's probably counter-adaptive - putting the organism at risk to predators. The brain is better at a "peek-a-boo" strategy for detection. The following four processes reflect the value of down time:

Internal

Long-lasting learning is generated from going "internal." We can take information in better when it's not forced on us by an outsider; and when we can process it in our own way.

Indirect

Much of our learning is non-direct instruction or nonconscious acquisition. For example, little Johnny learns very quickly to maintain a low profile when Daddy comes home drunk. He learns this adaptation behavior without formal instruction in the subject; and it is a lesson that, though unconsciously absorbed, is deeply imbedded.

Rest

Neural fixing only happens with no stimuli or non-competing stimuli.

Wait time

Clinical studies suggest that it takes up to six hours for any skill or action based learning to "imprint."

This principle suggests we ought to integrate movement, activities, and games into economics, mathematics, and accounting (or whatever) in the same way a coach has players count, think, plan, and react.

Wait!

Take a break! Hope you are enjoying the journey...What are your thoughts and feelings about
"down time?"

Principle #8:
Patterns Drive Understanding

Intelligence is the ability to elicit and to construct useful patterns. How do you deal with this reality in a practical way?

What's the first thing you noticed about the following groups of geometrical figures?

Did you notice how the groups of figures were *different* or how they were the *same*, or how they followed a *pattern*? Though this is a simple example, it underscores our brain's hunger for meaning. In its search for meaning, the brain seeks patterns, associations, and connections with the new data and data previously stored. Each pattern that is discovered can then be added to the learner's "perceptual maps", at which time the brain finds relief from the state of confusion, anxiety, or stress that accompanies raw data.

There are many ways to encourage learning through pattern formation. The following suggestions reflect just a few:

- Days or weeks before starting a topic, pre-expose learners to the lesson with oral previews, applicable games, metaphorical descriptions, and posted mind-maps or outlines of the topic.

- Before beginning a topic, give global overviews using transparencies, videos, handouts, or posters.

- Encourage students to discuss their learning in an unstructured, as well as structured format. Form groups or dyads for activities that encourage dialogue and teamwork. Activities might include the creation of mind-maps or a model or picture of what students are learning. Allow time for free-form conversation, as well.

- At the close of a unit or lesson, allow students to evaluate the pros and cons of the learning, discuss the relevance of it, and demonstrate their patterning with models, plays, peer teaching, etc.

Discover how each "puzzle piece" is part of something larger - its relationship to the whole - the "big picture". Isolated information has little meaning. Our brains build larger patterns to help us form genuine structures of meaning.

This principle suggests that we ought to be aware of how the brain makes sense out of random information through pattern-making; and the importance of engaging the learner with a big picture perspective.

Principle #9:
Drive for Meaning

Meaning is more critical to the brain than information. In what ways do you help ensure meaning-making?

The brain is generally poor at learning random data and isolated facts. It constantly seeks to make sense out of what is happening. Your students don't really want information; they want meaning. The search to make meaning out of our lives seems to be innate. Until *you* understand what makes meaning, you can't help *them* get it. We gain meaning three ways: patterns, emotions, and relevance. We learn best with context, the big picture, real-life learning, and interdisciplinary relationships. When things are emotional, they are assigned more meaning, too.

The brain naturally seeks meaning. As learning catalysts, we can either impede or facilitate that process. The primary variables are:

Relevance
Connect information with other known information. Use associations with prior knowledge to make it meaningful.

Emotion
The stronger the emotion, the more the meaning. Emotional experiences "code" our learning as important.

Context/Patterns
Information in isolation has little meaning. Each "puzzle piece" is always part of something larger. Meaning comes from understanding the larger pattern. Some examples include community service work, neighborhood issues, health, romance, eliciting, past experiences, and complex real-life projects.

This principle suggests that we create conditions for meaning-making.

Principle #10:
Nonconscious Learning

We process both parts and wholes simultaneously.
We are affected by a great deal of peripheral influences.

How is this reality addressed in your learning environment, instructional practices, and curriculum?

Surprisingly, a great deal of what we learn and what we know is not taught to us. It is simply "picked up." The process of acquisition allows for vast amounts of material to influence us through our senses.

Since our brain is designed to pay attention to only one sense at a time, the other inputs exert a significant cumulative influence on our learning. We learn to speak our native language mostly by just picking it up. We learned how to do our job by trial and error, role-models, inferences, and countless conscious and nonconscious influences. Sometimes, as a teacher, you just have to get out of the way of learning. Don't try to control, modulate, restrict, channel, or manipulate it so much. Set it up and let it happen. Encourage projects that guide the student's learning. The underlying principle here is to not *force* learning, but to *orchestrate* it.

This principle makes the case for less direct instruction and more orchestrated learning. We also ought to actively pursue orchestration of learning through rituals, cultural and social celebration, acknowledgment, teamwork, posters, plants, and natural lighting.

Principle #11:
The Social Brain

Intelligence is valued in the context of the society we live in. The brain develops better in concert with others.

How do you incorporate this principle into your curriculum?

Our brain cannot be good at everything; therefore, it selects over time that which will ensure its survival. As a species, the human brain has evolved to use language as our primary means for communication. This may partly explain why groups, teams, and cooperative learning benefit our understanding and application of new concepts; group work requires us to communicate with each other. Through this process, learning seems to be enhanced. The natural tendency for both children and adults in a learning environment, free of threat, is to talk in class. A great deal of learning takes place by talking to each other - exchanging emotions and feelings, sharing, discussion, brainstorming, and problem-solving.

This principle suggests we ought to orchestrate learning environments that use more teams, pairings, and re-groupings to maximize learning.

Principle #12:
Complex and Adaptive System

Every brain adapts to its environment based on experience. Effective teaching and impactful change involves consideration of the entire complex system.

In what ways do you address the process of learning system-wide?

- Different areas of the brain develop and mature at different rates. We develop our "fight or flight" capacity first, and our problem-solving skills last.

- Most areas of our brain are accessed on a daily basis. This happens because our brain has already pruned away the neurons it doesn't need. Your brain has been personally customizing itself for you since the day you were born. It has been designed to fit your life so naturally that it "grows" to the "size" you need it to be. The idiom, "Use it or lose it" fits here. The more you use your brain, the more it expands.

- The brain is highly adaptive, especially in the early years of life. Severe damage to either hemisphere will usually be compensated for by the other hemisphere if the damage occurs early (before five years). After that, the switch-over ability is reduced.

- The brain alters it's receptor sites for receiving neurotransmitters based on the environment. In an excessively stressed or threatening situation, the brain will increase receptor sites for noradrenaline. This adaptation may result in more aggressive, impulsive behaviors. Similarly, in males, the role of "top dog" or leader actually boosts testosterone production. Interestingly, it is the leadership role that inspires the increased hormone level, rather than the increased hormones influencing the individual's role. Serotonin levels are likely to drop with an increase in social status and increase with reduced status.

- Languages (especially foreign ones!) ought to be learned before leaving elementary school. After age 10, the brain "self-prunes" and many neurons (brain cells) dedicated for language are reallocated or absorbed back into the system.

To what degree does our brain change over time? We can all see for ourselves how different an infant's brain is from an adolescent's. The brain develops on different, but normal, timetables which can be one to three years apart in early developmental stages. We've all formed a lifetime of habits - some good, some bad. Just how much can we change by the time were adults? Probably more than you realize.

Every brain is unique because it develops in it's own unique world and adapts in response to its environment. The brain excels at adaptation. As a result, each brain modifies itself in response to things that others haven't had to adapt to. It's the adaptation that makes us intelligent. Single-answer, one-way learning and testing makes little sense. Humans have survived by problem-solving and flexible thinking. Schools ought to reflect this necessary adaptation. Our brain keeps growing new dendrites as long as we provide it with novel experiences, learner-controlled feedback, and appropriate challenge.

This principle suggests we ought to utilize more variety in our methodology and more learner choice in the learning process.

Walk The Talk:
Brain-Compatible Curriculum

Includes:

- Developmentally-appropriate lesson plans and strategies
- Culturally-appropriate (general and specific) lessons
- Integrated and interdisciplinary material
- Lessons relevant to students and teacher
- Awareness of gender differences
- Social and emotional literacy
- Nutritional information
- Early music training
- Learning-to-learn skills
- Daily physical activity
- Metacognition strategies
- Drug/toxin awareness

All of these curriculum concepts are made relevant through the skills of the facilitator and the student's own initiative.

REST STOP

Reflection and Processing Time...

What do you think? Are there ways you can implement brain-compatible strategies in your classroom? What are they?

_____

_____

_____

_____

_____

_____

_____

_____

_____

_____

40 Ways to Boost Motivation:
in a Brain-Compatible Way

Incorporate:

- Immediate Success
- Personal/Relevant
- Confusion
- Hands-On Learning
- Novelty
- Brain-Gym/Cross Laterals
- Celebrations
- Physical Movement
- Success Stories
- Greater Likelihood Of Success
- Stories/Metaphors
- Context Beliefs Improved
- Challenges
- Right Learning Styles
- The "Right State"
- Set Passionate Goals
- Capability Beliefs
- Health/Fitness To Learn
- Increased Feedback
- Positive Peer Pressure
- Curiosity

- Role-Model Motivation
- Music
- Demonstrations
- Make It OK To Make Mistakes
- Learners Share Successes
- Accountability
- Strong Reasons Why
- More Choice
- Lower Stress
- Access To Resources
- Meeting Their Values
- Know You Make A Difference
- Role Model Joy Of Learning
- Reduce The Pain Of Failure
- Make The Learning Fun
- Build Rapport First
- Address Fears and Barriers
- Set Learners Up To Win
- Teach Learners How They Learn

Avoid Rewards!

Over the long-term, studies suggest rewards:

- Reduce intrinsic motivation.
- Cheapen value and love of learning.
- Give the wrong messages.
- Create an escalating no-win game.

Alternatives to Rewards:

- Increase feedback, and celebrations.
- Role-model joy of learning and discovery.
- Provide more acknowledgments, choice, control, and novelty.

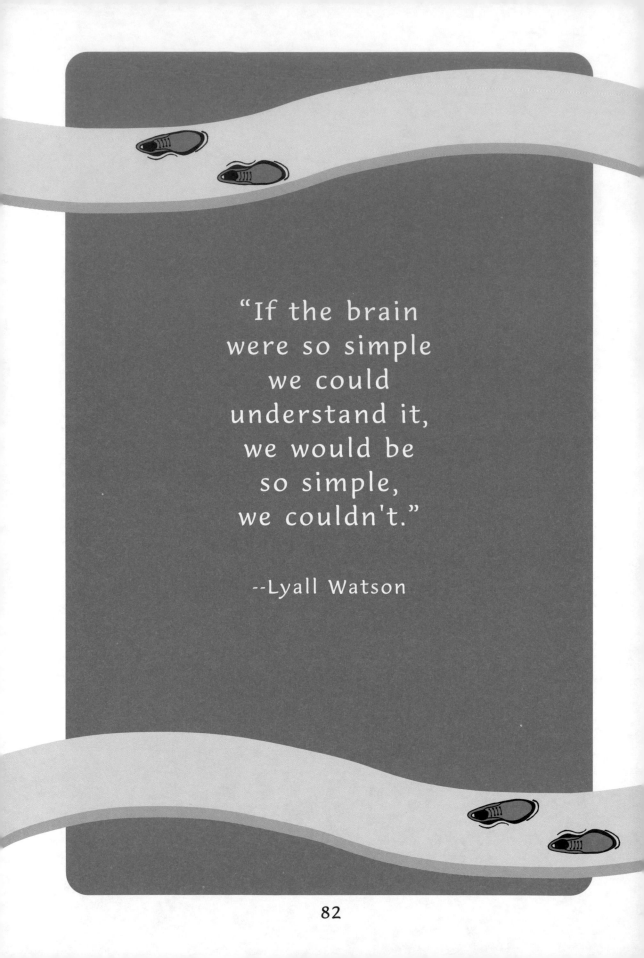

"If the brain
were so simple
we could
understand it,
we would be
so simple,
we couldn't."

--Lyall Watson

Trail Guide to Greater Transformation:
Section 3

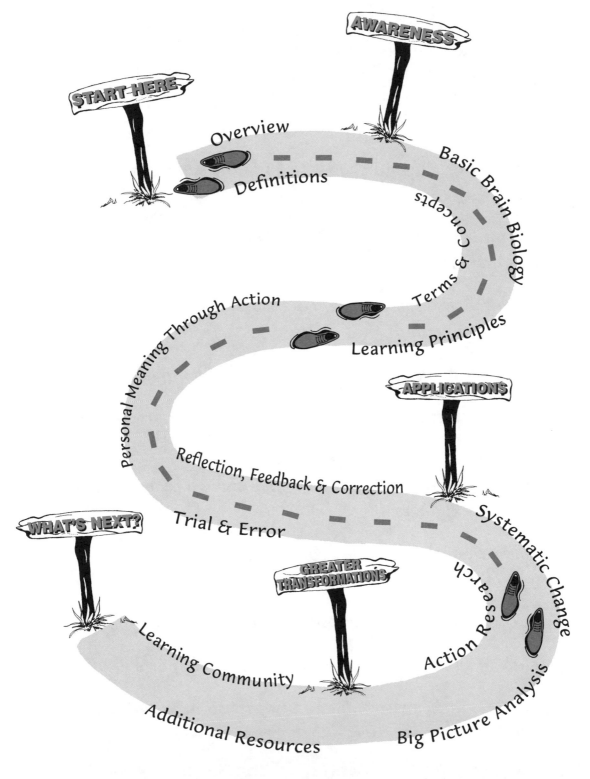

START HERE

AWARENESS

Overview

Definitions

Basic Brain Biology

Terms & Concepts

Personal Meaning Through Action

Learning Principles

APPLICATIONS

Reflection, Feedback & Correction

Systematic Change

WHAT'S NEXT?

Trial & Error

GREATER TRANSFORMATIONS

Action Research

Learning Community

Big Picture Analysis

Additional Resources

Systemic Change:
the Next Level

L et's say, you've successfully implemented brain-compatible learning into your own curriculum and you would like to see the same success implemented school or system-wide. Some of the potential challenges you may come up against are:

- *Other staff may not choose to go in the same direction you have.*

- *A staff member may have had a bad experience that left a bad taste in their mouth.*

- *A staff member may not grasp the relevancy; or is uninspired by the new paradigm.*

- *Other staff may fear it will invalidate their past work.*

- *Lack of parent, school board, administrative, or community support.*

- *Staff may feel that they don't have enough down time to make the changes.*

- *There are too many other conflicting priorities and programs.*

- *Lack of feedback or accountability stymies the process.*

- *Lack of sufficient resources or follow-up impairs process.*

- *Staff get disheartened due to insufficient acknowledgment and lack of celebration.*

Big Picture Analysis:
Transformation Happens

Transformation can occur on many levels: individual, social, cultural, political, and system-wide. Sometimes it even happens without us knowing. Once you transform your own environment and philosophy and are walking the talk on a daily and moment-by-moment basis, others can't help but take notice. Just as the snowball gets bigger rolling downhill, so will the awareness of brain-compatible learning. What works gets imbedded. Though change usually happens gradually, it surely occurs. Though our brain is poorly designed to take on whole new paradigms at once, it is well designed for "nibbling away" at a concept or building a model over time. Expect systemic change to take time. Meanwhile, you can continue to make gains by:

- *Identifying your own individual beliefs.*
- *Identifying limiting institutional practices.*
- *Redesigning the purpose, approach, content and processes in your own curriculum.*
- *Applying your learning; doing your own action research.*
- *Doing big picture analysis and long-term planning.*
- *Remembering that meaningful transformation takes time.*

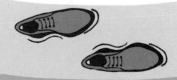

Action Research
Makes a Difference!

Action research means applying your knowledge about brain-compatible learning to your own classroom or learning environment. In so doing, remember to keep the following areas in mind:

Instruction

Are your teaching approaches flexible, individualized, based on multiple learning styles, novel, and interesting? Do you ask students to work in teams? Are your assignments fun, realistic, complex and rich? Do you insure that students receive lots of feedback on a daily basis?

Curriculum

Is your subject matter relevant, cross-curricular, interdisciplinary, and stage appropriate? Is it examined from many angles over a period of time? Do you present the big picture, as well as the smaller chunks? Is there an emphasis on the process - on learning to learn? Do you include life-skills learning and emotional literacy?

Environment

Is your classroom set up with a variety of seating and temperature options? Do you use music, multiple lighting types, rich visuals and aromas? Do you have plants in your classroom? If you have classroom pets, are they well cared for? Does your classroom maintain a rule of respect for all individuals; and an environment free of threat and tight teacher control?

Assessment

Does your assessment approach take into consideration the uniqueness of the individual learner? Do you assess learning over time, rather than incrementally? Do you include emotional literacy and multiple intelligences in the assessment process? Do you set up structures for peer and personal assessment? Have you eliminated traditional tests, comparisons and curves? Do you emphasize mental models and give learners some choice in the assessment process?

How might you use your classroom to conduct your own action research?

_____

_____

_____

_____

_____

_____

_____

_____

_____

Reflection and Processing Time...

In what ways do you already apply the principles of brain compatible learning? Can you think of other strategies in the following categories that you would like to try?

Instruction

_____

_____

Curriculum

_____

_____

Environment

_____

_____

Assessment

_____

_____

The Learning Community

Schools or "learning communities" that use brain-compatible learning methods outlined in this book are consistently more successful than those that don't. What is meant by successful? There are fewer dropouts, the students enjoy school more, they are willing to take risks, think for themselves, and be creative. They understand how they learn and love to do it. It's more than just applying a few techniques. A school must become a learning organization. In the process of transforming your school into a learning community, consider the following "share-holders":

Parents

Have you "brought the parents in" to what you are doing? Do they understand the basic principles of brain-compatible learning? Are they seeing the results of your efforts? Are they being asked to get involved in the classroom as perhaps a guest speaker, volunteer, or contributor? Encourage family support, positive parental feedback, academic involvement, and a home environment that is rich with opportunities for exploration and managed risk.

Teachers

Are you nurturing teachers to support each other? Does every teacher know every other teacher's best ideas? Are you open to their suggestions, feedback, and questions? Are formal and informal structures of support in place? Are you building a collective vision?

Students

Are students included in the decision-making process? Are you providing an environment that is responsive to their goals? Are students allowed to move around freely in the classroom and to work in pairs or groups if they wish? Are students always respected as an important part of the learning organization?

Local Media

Have you notified the various media to elicit stories about your classroom or school? Perhaps, you could you invite them to an open house, or a presentation of special term projects, a school-wide event, or a guest speaker.

School and District Staff

Have you asked your school and district administrators how they think the current system works, and how they think teaching and learning works in their area of responsibility? Have you shared your learning with them? Are they familiar with brain-compatible learning strategies? Would they like to learn more? Keep asking "why" until you find out what investment your organization has in keeping a particular useless policy in place.

A learning organization of the twenty-first century will not necessarily know the best way to do everything; what it will know, however, is how to learn its way into the future. Educators will be committed to the process of making their environments brain-compatible, rather than brain-antagonistic. Staff will feel free to speak honestly and to share ideas; there will be respect for differences; teachers will enjoy their profession; and they will delight in their students' success. Does this sound like a place you would like to work? Keep reading!

What's Next?

Fortunately, we have enough insights to make dramatic and powerful changes in how we conceptualize, plan and implement educational policy today. While the research doesn't always give us the specific form or structure for how to shift the paradigm, it's clear that we have enough to figure it out ourselves. Naturally, a book like this is not meant to be the end-all; and it will need to be updated every few years. The discoveries are coming so fast that even the professionals who study this field full-time are overwhelmed. But don't wait for more research. The research will just keep coming. It makes more sense to start with what you can do today and take the next step - your own action research. In that process, there are plenty of additional resources for you to reference along the way (please see appendix).

Good luck as you continue the journey into the brain and how it learns best. And congratulations on completing the first leg of this exciting journey.

Trail Guide:
Congratulations, you've finished!

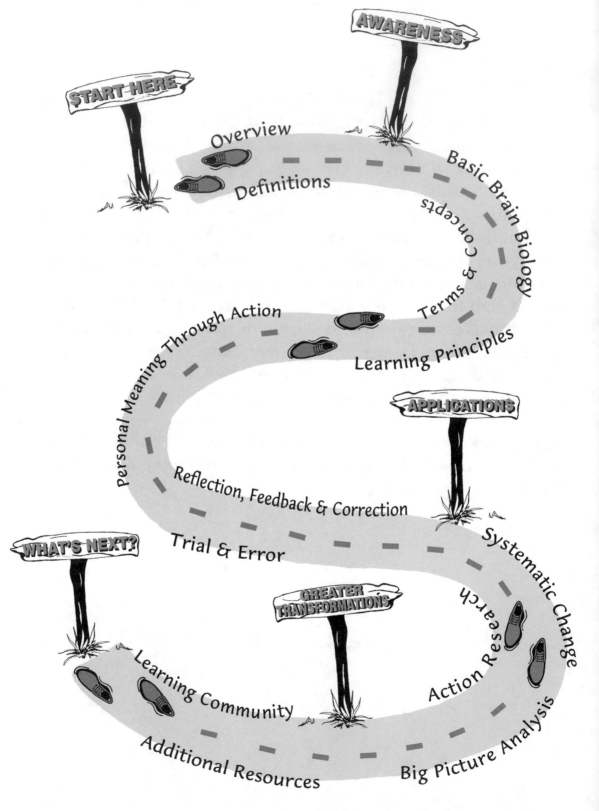

AWARENESS

START HERE

Overview

Definitions

Basic Brain Biology

Terms & Concepts

Personal Meaning Through Action

Learning Principles

APPLICATIONS

Reflection, Feedback & Correction

WHAT'S NEXT?

Trial & Error

Systematic Change

GREATER TRANSFORMATIONS

Action Research

Learning Community

Additional Resources

Big Picture Analysis

Appendix

Take the Next Step:
Brain-Smart Resources & Support

Other Books by Eric Jensen:

Brain-Compatible Strategies

Get over 500 easy-to-use classroom strategies that purposely engage the brain to boost attention, motivation, learning, meaning, and transfer.

Brain-Based Learning

The most complete volume on new approaches to discipline, intelligence, memory, attention, learning and environments, etc. A highly detailed and practical book for all teachers, administrators, and trainers. Fully referenced, easy to use and well illustrated.

Completing the Puzzle

Especially for new teachers and administrators. Quick reading, cuts right to the heart of the matter, specific and highly practical.

The Learning Brain

Key brain research on nutrition, learning states, attention, music, gender, motivation, physical activity, environments, color, thinking, intelligences, prenatal, toxins, plants, aging, and memory.

SuperTeaching

Over 1,000 practical strategies for energizers, discipline, openings, closings, environments, multiple intelligences, and brain research. Enough ideas for 3 years!

Other Recommended Reading:

Celebration of Neurons by Robert Sylwester

The subtitle is an educator's guide to the human brain. It is just that--a detailed summary of the brain and how it learns and reacts to attention, learning and memory. Excellent & well-researched.

ITI: The Model by Susan Kovalik
The best book out on the brain-based curriculum. Effortlessly weaves brain research with curriculum with environments. Practical and complete.

Unleashing the Power of Perceptual Change by Renate and Geoffrey Caine
A new release by these ground-breaking authors continues their explorations into the brain and learning by unveiling perceptual orientations or different views of reality that frame the way people perceive education.

Smart Moves by Carla Hannaford
An excellent overview of the body-mind relationship. Easy-to-understand and written for all levels, especially the introductory level. Best book on educational kinesiology (EK).

The Learning Revolution by Gorden Dryden and Jeanette Vos
The best collection of school success stories and practical learning strategies in years--a kind of encyclopedic, 90s version of Rose's Accelerated Learning.

Owner's Manual for the Brain by Pierce Howard
Here's a practical guide to everything you wanted to know about your brain. Especially strong in gender differences, stress, attention and memory. A must-buy for all brain-owners.

Seeing With Magic Glasses by Launa Ellison
Written by a teacher who is currently implementing brain-based principles. She talks about her struggles and successes in a way every teacher can appreciate. Excellent.

Other Brain-Friendly Resources:

Bright Brain Video Program by Eric Jensen
A learning readiness stimulator video program for kids ages 4 to 8 and a teacher's activity book called "Bright Brain Activities" for active learning.

Brain-Based Learning and Teaching Video Program
Get this full-length, two-video set complete with special effects and in-depth interviews. Perfect for staff development.

Brain-Compatible Workshops and Trainings: The author conducts workshops and in-depth programs on brain-compatible teaching and learning. These practical development programs are cost-efficient, long-lasting, and provide in-house resources for your school or district. Call (800) 63-TRAIN for free information and a preview video. Training Certification available.

Learning Brain Expo: This exciting 3-day conference is held each winter in San Diego. See, hear, and experience dozens of the world's top experts linking new brain research with learning, thinking, enrichment, arts, memory, curriculum, physical education, assessment, movement, and music. Highly recommended! Call (800) 63-TRAIN for details.

For a FREE catalog with over 150 brain-compatible resources including videos, audio tapes, software, books, posters, etc. contact: The Brain Store, Inc. San Diego, CA 92121; or call: (800) 325-4769 or (619) 546-7555; or fax: (619) 546-7560; or E-Mail: edubrain@connectnet.com.

Brain Glossary

Acetylcholine - A common neurotransmitter, particularly involved in long term memory formation. Specifically released at neuromuscular junctions, it's present at higher levels during rest and sleep.

ACTH - Also called corticotrophin, this stress-related hormone is produced by the pituitary gland. It's released into your system when you experience injury, emotion, pain, infections or other trauma.

Adrenaline - Under stress, fear, or excitement, this hormone is released from your adrenal gland into your bloodstream. When it reaches your liver, it stimulates the release of glucose for rapid energy. Abrupt increases caused by anger can constrict heart vessels, requiring the heart to pump with higher pressure. Also known as epinephrine.

Amygdala - Located in the middle of the brain, this almond-shaped complex of related nuclei is a critical processor area for senses. Connected to the hippocampus, it plays a role in emotionally-laden memories. Contains huge number of opiate receptor sites implicated in rage, fear, and sexual feelings.

Axons - These are the long fibers extending from the brain cells (neurons) that carry the output (an electrical nerve impulse) to other neurons. Can be up to a meter long. There is just one per neuron, but they can subdivide to connect with many dendrites. When used often enough, axons build up a fatty white insulation called myelin.

Brain Stem - Located at the top of the spinal cord. Links the lower brain with the middle of the brain and cerebral hemispheres. Often referred to as the lower brain.

Broca's Area - Part of the frontal lobe in the cerebrum. It converts thoughts into sounds (or written words) and sends the message to the motor area. Impulses go first to Wernicke's area, then to Broca's area.

Cerebellum - A cauliflower-shaped structure located below the occipital area and next to the brainstem. The word is Latin for "little brain." Traditionally, research linked it to balance, posture, coordination and muscle movements. Newer research has linked it to cognition, novelty and emotions.

Cerebral Cortex - This is the newspaper-sized, 1/4" thick, outermost layer of the cerebrum. It's wrinkled, six layers deep, and packed with brain cells (neurons). Cortex is the Latin word for "bark" or "rind."

Cerebrum - This is the largest part of the brain, composed of the left and right hemisphere. It contains frontal, parietal, temporal and occipital lobes.

Cingulate Gyrus - This structure lies directly above the corpus callosum. It mediates communication between the cortex and mid-brain structures.

Corpus Callosum - A white-matter bundle of millions of nerve fibers which connect the left and right hemisphere. Located in the mid-brain area.

Dendrites - These are the strand-like fibers emanating from the cell body. Similar to spider webs or cracks in the wall, they are the receptor sites for axons when they connect to make a synapse. Each cell usually has many, many dendrites.

Dopamine - A powerful and common neurotransmitter primarily involved in producing a positive mood or feeling. Secreted by neurons in the substantia nigra, mid brain, and hypothalamus, it plays a role in movements, too. It's commonly in shortage in patients suffering from Parkinson's Disease.

Endorphin - A natural opiate, this neurotransmitter is similar to morphine. It is produced in the pituitary gland and protects against excessive pain. It is released with ACTH and enkephalins into the brain.

Enkephalin - This morphine-like substance consists of five opiate-type amino acids. Released into the brain with ACTH and endorphins to combat pain.

Frontal Lobes - One of four main areas of the cerebrum, the upper brain area. Controls voluntary movement, verbal expression, problem-solving, will power, and planning. The other three areas of the cerebrum are the occipital, parietal and temporal.

GABA - Gamma-aminobutyric acid, this common neurotransmitter acts as an inhibitory agent, an "off" switch.

Glial - A non-neuronal cell, these are one of two major types of brain cells (the other is a neuron). These outnumber neurons 10 to 1, and are also known as interneurons. They carry nutrients, speed repair, and may form their own communication network. Short for "neuroglia."

Hippocampus - Found deep in the temporal lobe, central to the middle of the brain area. It is crescent-shaped, and strongly involved in learning and memory formation.

Hypothalamus - Located in the bottom center of the middle area of the brain. Complex thermostat-like structure that influences and regulates appetite, hormone secretion, digestion, sexuality, circulation, emotions, and sleep.

Lateralization - Refers to the activity of using one hemisphere more than another. The term "relative lateralization" is more accurate since we are usually using at least some of the left and right hemisphere at the same time.

Limbic System - An older term coined by Paul MacLean in 1952. This is a group of connected structures in the mid brain area which include the hypothalamus, amygdala, thalamus, fornix, hippocampus, and cingulate gyrus.

Lower Brain - This is the lower portion of the brain composed of the upper spinal cord, medulla, pons and some say, the reticular formation. It sorts sensory information and regulates our survival functions like breathing and heart rate.

Medulla - Located in the brain stem, it channels information between the cerebral hemispheres and the spinal cord. It controls respiration, circulation, wakefulness, breathing, and heart rate.

Myelin - A fatty white shield that coats and insulates axons. They can help make the cells (neurons) more efficient and travel up to 12 times faster. Habits may be a result of myelinated axons.

Norepinephrine - (also known as noradrenaline) A common neurotransmitter, primarily involved in our arousal states: fight or flight, metabolic rate, blood pressure, emotions, and mood.

Neurons - One of two types of brain cells. We have about 100 billion of these. Receives stimulation from its branches known as dendrites. Communicates to other neurons by firing a nerve impulse along an axon.

Neurotransmitters - Our brain's biochemical messengers. We have over 50 types of them. These usually act as the stimulus that excites a neighboring neuron or an inhibitor to suppress activation.

Occipital Lobe - Located in the rear of the cerebrum. One of the four major areas of the upper brain, this processes our vision. The other three areas are parietal, frontal and temporal lobes.

Oxytocin - A peptide also know as the "commitment molecule." It's released during sex and pregnancy and influences "unlearning" and pair bonding.

Parietal Lobe - The top of our upper brain, it's one of four major areas of the cerebrum. This area deals with reception of sensory information from the contralateral body side. It also plays a part in reading, writing language, and calculation. The other three lobes are the occipital, temporal and frontal.

Pons - Located near the top of the brain stem, above the medulla. It's a critical relay station for our sensory information.

Reticular Formation - A small structure, located at the top of the brain stem and bottom of mid-brain area. It's the regulator responsible for attention, arousal, sleep-awake states, and consciousness.

Serotonin - A common neurotransmitter, most responsible for inducing relaxation, regulating mood and sleep. Antidepressants (like Prozac) usually suppress the absorption of serotonin, making it more active.

Synapse - It's the junction point when neurons connect. When an axon of one neuron releases neurotransmitters to stimulate the dendrites of another cell, the resulting spot where the reaction occurs is a synapse. The adult human has trillions of synapses.

Temporal Lobes - Located on the side of the cerebrum (in the middle of our upper brain, near our ears), it's an area believed responsible for hearing, senses, listening language, learning and memory storage. The other three major cerebrum areas are the frontal, occipital and parietal lobes.

Thalamus - Located deep within the middle of the brain, it is a key sensory relay station. It's also part of the body's reward system.

Vasopressin - A stress-related hormone that is partly responsible for our aggression.

Wernicke's Area - The upper back edge of the temporal lobe. Here the brain converts thoughts into language.

Index

About the Author

A former teacher, Eric Jensen has taught at all levels of education - from elementary though university. He's listed in "Who's Who Worldwide" and is a former Outstanding Young Man of America selection. In 1981, Jensen co-founded SuperCamp, the nation's first and largest brain-compatible learning program for teens, now with over 20,000 graduates. He's authored *Student Success Secrets*, *Brain-Based Learning*, *Brain-Compatible Strategies*, *Completing the Puzzle*, *Teaching With the Brain In Mind*, *The Learning Brain*, and *SuperTeaching*. He remains deeply committed to making a positive, significant, lasting difference in the way the world learns. Jensen, a member of the international Society of Neuroscience, currently speaks at conferences and does trainings and consulting internationally. To contact him, call or write:

Jensen Learning Corp.
(888) 63-TRAIN
Box 2551, Del Mar, California 92014 USA